ULTIMATE
FUTSAL
DEFENDER

TACTICS EXPLAINED SIMPLY

BY Artyom samoylov

INTRODUCTION

There are several factors, which make a defensive player act one way or another. First off all it's the **location** of the ball. Second - **positioning** of opponents and team mates on the pitch. Third - the **status** of an opponent (with the ball, without the ball, about to receive the ball etc.)

This book is structured in a way, so the reader could be getting into all the details of individual defensive actions **step by step**. The main focus of this book is **individual defensive actions**. In my opinion, this is the topic to start from, when learning about defensive actions in futsal. Next books of this series will be concentrating on other defensive aspects (such as team defense, for example).

In each section for the book we will be concentrating on main tactical aspects, then - on small nuances. Each section will also provide illustrated examples for better understanding of the topic. Last by not the least - in those cases, where it is necessary, I will provide additional exercises, so you could get better by practicing certain things.

This book has three main sections:
1. **Opponent without the ball**
2. **Opponent is about to receive the ball (the ball is already moving towards a player, but he yet to make a contact with it)**
3. **Opponent is already has the ball in his possession**

In addition to these three blocks of information, we will also talk about **special scenarios**. But let's not rush into anything and take it slowly.

By the way, I would recommend to work with this book without any hurry, but instead - take it topic by topic. This way the material will be absorbed way better. In the future you will be able to get back to certain parts of this book as soon as you have certain problem.

Have fun and enjoy the reading!

OPPONENT WITHOUT THE BALL

MAIN PRINCIPLES

I would like to start with an explanation of how I use some terms in this book. To me there is no defenders or attackers in futsal, because these are positions. Futsal has no nominal positions (I talk about this in details in my book series "Stupid futsal mistakes") except a goal-keeper. All field players have to play on the same level in any sector of the pitch. Therefore futsal players are universal. They have to be at least. Professionals are.

Therefore I separate players not by their positions, but by their **functions**. So to me there can be no defender, but instead - there is defensive player. The one, who is (at the moment) a player of a team, which doesn't have a possession of the ball. **Defensive player is the one, who performs defensive actions, when his opponent's team has the ball.**

In this book though, I will be using the term "defender" just to make it easier for you, my reader. But you have to remember, that when I say "defender", I mean - a player of a team, which hasn't got the ball.

So let's dive in. In order to understand, how to defend against an opponent with the ball, first of all we have to know, how to behave in **situations leading** to that. Defender has to be able to read the game well and have the necessary knowledge to **evaluate** the situation and act according to it.

For example, a defender has to know, what is the right moment to get closer to his respective opponent or visa-versa - let him loose a bit. Defender also has to know, how and when he should be engaging in a fight for the ball or on the other hand - how and when to wait and contain his opposing player. In this section of the book we will be talking about all these aspects step-by-step.

Let's start with analyzing a couple of situations, so we could understand the best **positioning**, when playing against an **opponent without the ball**. We will learn to position ourselves in a so-called "**triangles**" and also - to choose the correct distance to respective opponents.

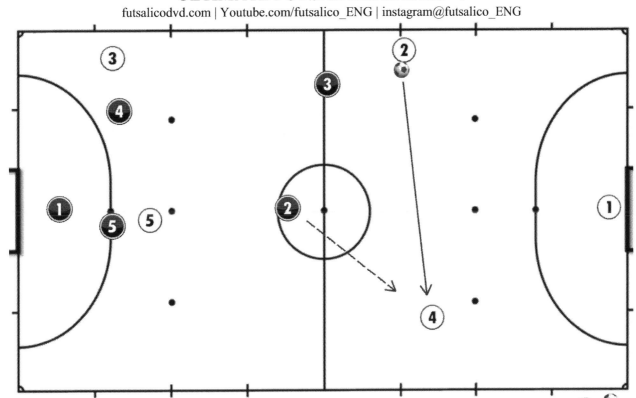

On the scheme above we can see the situation, where black nr.2 is responsible for white nr.4. Black nr.2 should not be leaving this position until the pass is played. He only start to move, when the pass is made and as soon as this happens black nr.2 has to be getting closer to his respective opponent. **Remember - we only move, when the ball moves!**

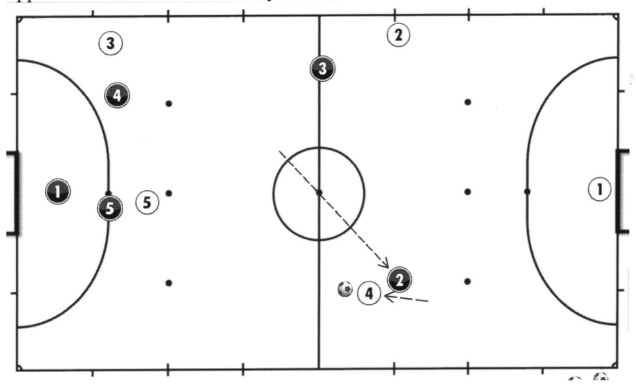

How close should black nr.2 get to white nr.4? If he gets too close, there is a risk, he is going to be outplayed. If a defender doesn't stop, when it's necessary, he is going to be outplayed. Outplayed easily on the counter-

futsalicodvd.com | Youtube.com/futsalico_ENG | instagram@futsalico_ENG

movement.

So what is the right way to do it? To make it easier for you to understand, I would like to give you a short formula or **algorithm of the correct actions**:

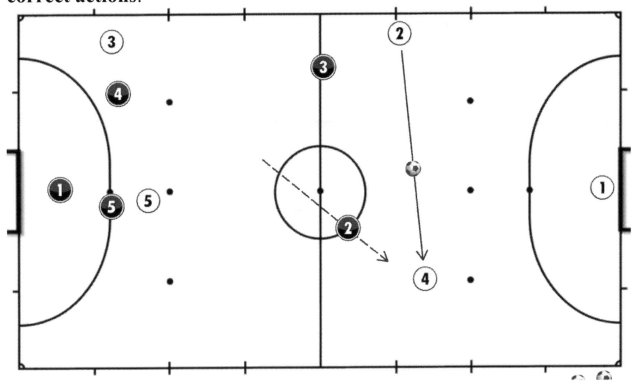

1. As long as the ball moves, defender should be as soon as possible reducing the distance between him and his respective player (scheme above).

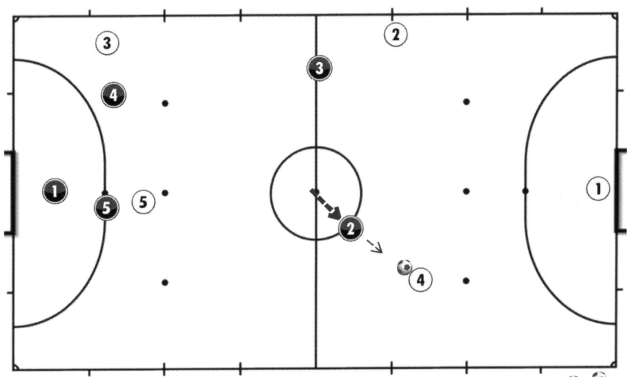

2. As soon as your respective player receives the ball, immediately

slower your movement.

Continue moving slowly and stop at the distance of 2m away from your respective opponent. If your opponent already received the ball and at this moment you are still further than 2 meters away from him, then keep reducing the distance very slowly and carefully - so you don't get outplayed.

Your **final (correct)** position:

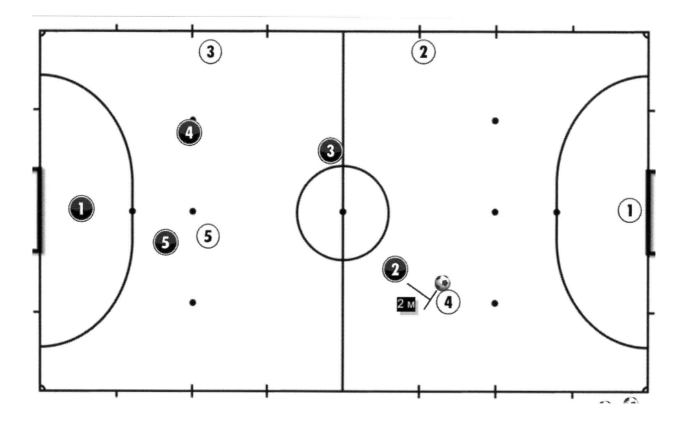

futsalicodvd.com | Youtube.com/futsalico_ENG | instagram@futsalico_ENG

POSITIONING ON THE PITCH

Now we know, when we should be moving and when we should be stopping. In this section of the book we will concentrate on the positioning against an opponent player without the ball. What is the right location on the pitch for a defender, who covers the opponent without the ball.

The rules is to be in the imaginary **triangle**, three points of which are - the ball, the center of your goal and your respective player (next scheme):

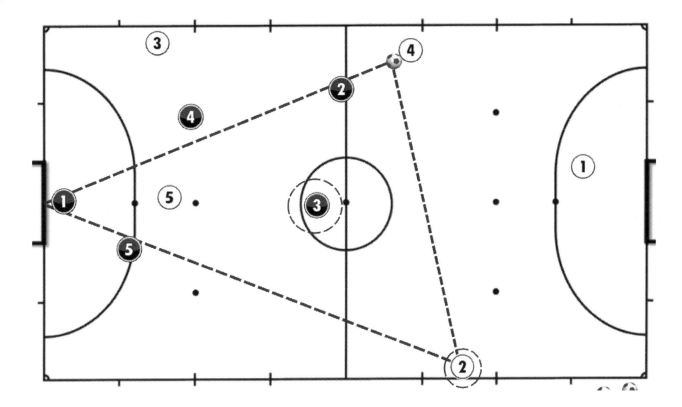

On the scheme above we can see the situation, where black nr.3 is covering white nr.2. You can also see the triangle, which is formed by the center of the goal, the ball and respective opponent. Black nr.3 is inside this triangle, so formally his positioning is correct. But where exactly should he position himself in this triangle?

In the next scheme you can see that there are **different possible variations** of movement for black nr.3. What should be the one to chose and what should be his final position?

If we talk about the tactic of zonal team defense, then black nr.3 should have positioned himself closer to the middle of our triangle. His main job would be to defend the middle zone - so no opponent moved into it freely and so there is no free passing line through it.

If it's the case with individual defense, then for a defender nr.3 it is not necessary to control the middle zone. His main responsibility in this case would be white nr.2. I am telling you this, so you understand, that positioning also varies depending on the system of defensive play. At the same moment there is one element, which is important in the any situation (regardless of the team tactic). This element (or aspect) should always be implemented. Regardless.

The rules of **peripheral vision** will be the one to guide you in any situation. IF futsal this term (peripheral vision) means the ability of a defender to see both things simultaneously - the ball and his respective player (player, who he is covering).

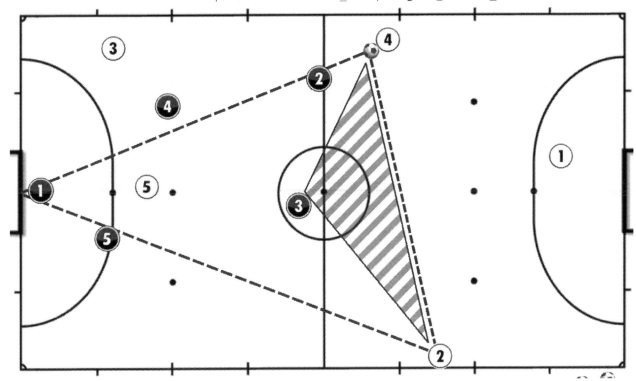

On the scheme above we can see the zone, which a defender should always (at any point of time) be able to see in this kind of situation. Certainly, I don't suggest, that defender's left eye should be turned to the left, while his right eye is turned to the right. I am saying, that a defender should be using his side (peripheral) vision to keep both the player with the ball and his respective played under control. Defender may be using slight turns of his head from time to time to adjust his positioning.

Remember, if as a defender you can not see simultaneously the player with the ball and the player, you are covering, that mean you have to adjust your positioning immediately. How you can do that? Do this:
1. Get down the pitch (towards your goal) a bit.
2. Turn your body a bit towards the side, which you cannot see.

In terms of our example, if black nr.3 loses the sight of white nr.2, then a defender should make a couple of steps towards his goal (not towards the right flank) and turn his body a bit to the right. Defender should stop at the point, when the control of both the ball and his opponent (white nr.2) is restored. This would be the correct **adjustment** of the positioning.

Let's now take a look at couple of another examples to make sure you understand the principles of defensive positioning even better. This time we will concentrate on the incorrect positioning inside the triangle!

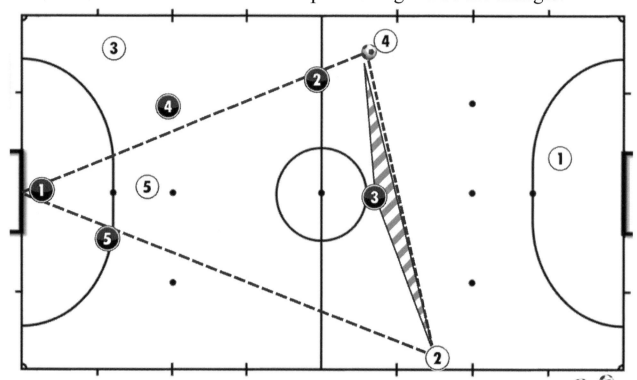

On the scheme above we can see, that defensive player nr.3 is located inside the triangle. That would be **correct**. On the other hand the angle or his sight is so big, that it will cause frequent loss of the control of either white n.2 or the ball.

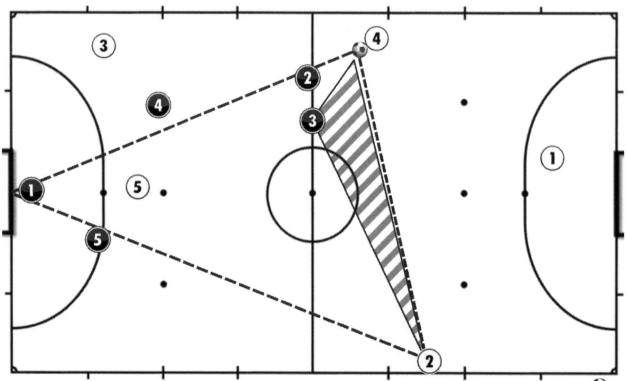

Similar incorrect positioning is shown on the scheme above. Again the angle is too big. In this position black nr.3 will have big problem controlling both the ball and white nr.2.

Here is another **extreme**:

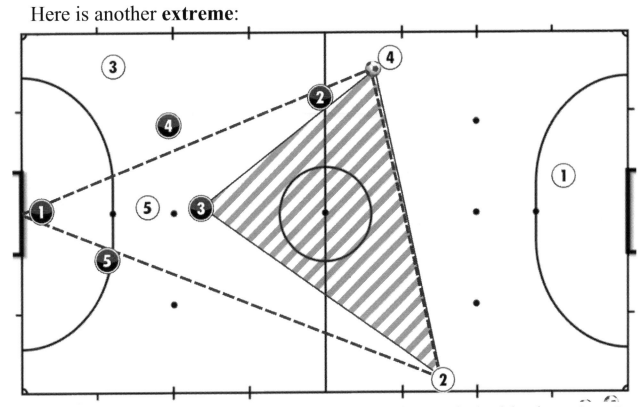

On the scheme above you can see that black nr.3 is inside the **triangle**. His sight angle is not big anymore. He can see both the ball and white nr.2. So what's the problem now, then? The problem is that we cannot say, that he keeps white nr.2 under his control. Therefore his contribution to overall team defensive structure and potential is minimal.

The reality is that white nr.2 is left out and can freely receive the ball, control it and start moving towards our goal (maybe even shoot). At the moment, when white nr.2 receives the ball, black nr.3 is going to be too far away.

futsalicodvd.com | Youtube.com/futsalico_ENG | instagram@futsalico_ENG

If from that position defender will start moving towards white nr.2, then when players meet, defender might be easily be outplayed on the counter movement. That reason for that is that white nr.2 would have way too much time to gain speed (next scheme).

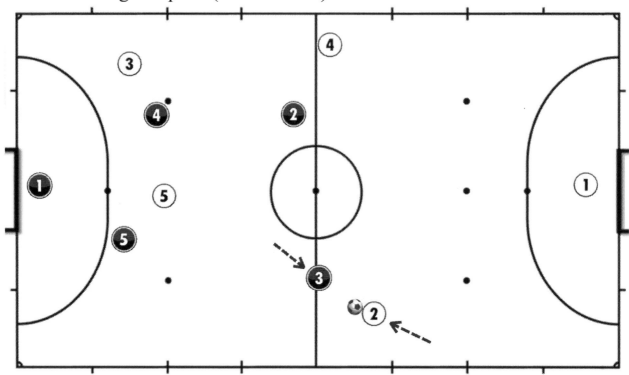

For example in personal cover tactic the ideal position of black nr.3 would be this one:

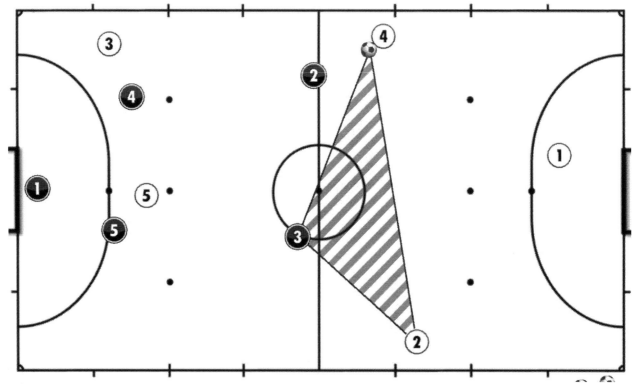

If it's a zonal defense tactics, then black nr.3 should position himself 2-3 steps to the left. It's necessary to not allow potentially dangerous pass

through the middle zone.

Second popular mistake in this case would be the incorrect position of the body. A defensive player should never turn his body to only one side: the ball side or player side. He should always and **simultaneously** be able to control both. Very often defensive players (when they find themselves in the position of black nr.2) locate themselves correctly in terms of their place on the pitch, but at the same time they look only one way: towards the respective player or towards the ball.

In the next scheme we can see the blind zone of black nr.3 in case, in the situation if **he looks only at the ball**:

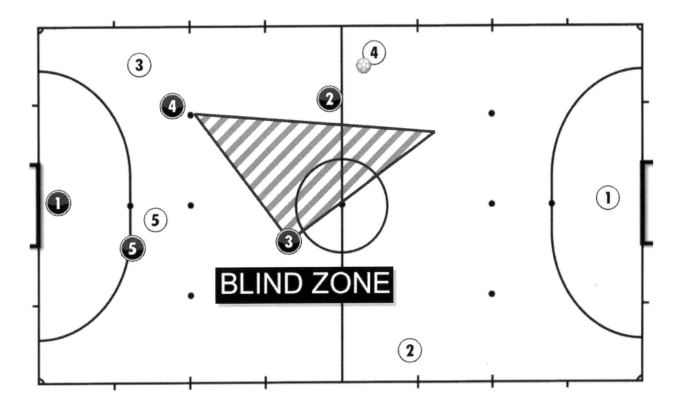

Here is a scheme (lower) of the same player, but when he looks only at his respective player and **totally ignores the ball**:

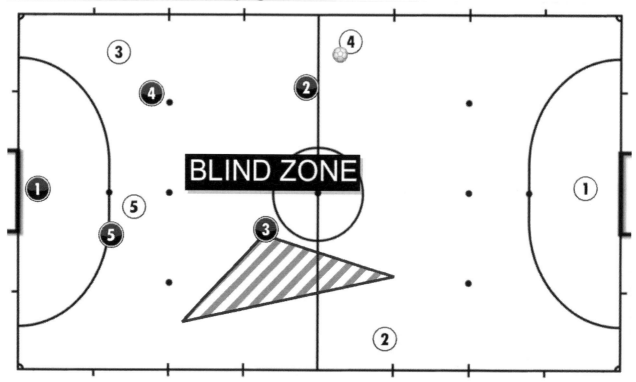

To sum-up, I can say that the defensive player's body should be turned in a manner, where he would be able to see both the ball and his respective player. His legs should be bent a bit and spread. This is necessary to keep the best body weight balance, because this would play a big part in defender's ability to react to any opponent's actions.

Here is a **good example** of what a body position should be like:

There is another very popular example of **ignoring the principles of peripheral vision:**

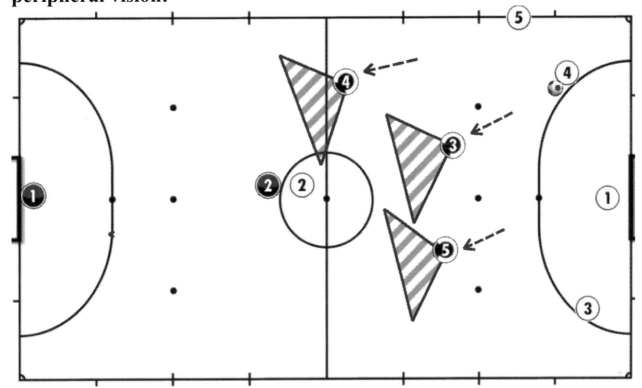

This often happens, when the team (in this case - black team) just lost the ball in attack and trying to shape a defensive formation. You can see, that black team's players immediately (after losing the ball) turn backwards and sprint "home" - in defense. This can only happen, if defending team's players totally **neglect** all defensive principles.

It's gets even worse if in this case a coach (captain, manager or player-coach) start shouting something like: "Back to defense! Immediately!". It get get even worse than that: if black nr.2 (the "last" player) also turns and goes back, totally leaving this respective opponent (white nr.2).

I call the nonsense behavior as a "blind retreat" or a panic. I talk in detail about cases of "blind retreat" in my series of books called **"Stupid futsal mistakes"**, which can be found on futsalicodvd.com. In the book, you are reading now, though, I would like to discuss the situation of "blind retreat" too, because it affects defender's actions.

This kind of retreat usually happens, when players think, that the effectiveness of their defensive actions depend on how fast they can "get back in defense" (to their half of the pitch). Player thinks, that the sooner they are on their half of the pitch, the better they can organize themselves. They also think, that the most important not to allow opponent to outrun defenders. It is important too, but it is not the most important in terms of effective defense.

This kind of thinking is not rational and in many cases is way less effective, than, for example, immediate pressure of the opponent (starting with the player with the ball) on his half of the pitch. If this pressure is applied with a good timing and knowledge, it an be very useful and stop opponent's attack in the beginning of it's development.

I am not suggesting, though, that you should always (!) apply pressure. I am saying, that you have to get ready to different scenarios and be able to read the game. The most important is to be able to understand, what is better a more effective: immediate pressure or quick (organized!) retreat.

A lot will **depend** on the positioning of a player with the ball, other opponents and whether defending team's player (closest to the ball) is able to immediately and effectively apply pressure on the opponent with the ball.

There is a **rule** (algorithm) of how to defend when the ball was just lost on opponent's half:

Closest defending team's player to the ball should make a **decision**: attack the player with the ball or allow him get hold of the ball. If opponent is allowed some freedom, then a defender should start a controlled retreat. What does it mean? It means always keep 2-3 meter distance between yourself (a defender) and attacking player. A defender should be **facing** an opponent with the ball (do not turn your back to him). Keep balance and get back while maintaining vision and control. Keep a certain body position, so most dangerous zones are under control too (we will talk in detail about this in the section called "space orientation" a bit later in this book).

On the scheme above you can see, that retreating players cannot see neither a ball, nor their respective opponents. Certainly in this situation there can be no conversation about controlling any zones. Black team is just panicking and fleeing. They have no information what so ever about what is going on on the pitch. They might as well just run straight into a shower.

SPACE ORIENTATION

In this section of the book we will analyze different situations, which often happen in a game. What we are going to be concentrating on is the location (positioning) of certain players in defense. I will be showing you some cases of **incorrect** defensive actions and tactical errors and also - will show you, how (and why) defenders should be positioning themselves.

It is going to be a detailed step-by-step explanation, therefore take this section of the book as the one, which you have to take your time with. Try to absorb the information slowly. I assure you, that when you reach the end of this chapter, you will reconsider your way of playing. You will know, how you should defend against your respective players individually and also - how a defense can be made effective **as a unit.**

In youth and also in amateur futsal the main reason of frequent defensive mistakes is usually the **overestimated** importance of the ball. Defenders are focusing on the ball for too much, forgetting about other game factors, such as opponent's players, zones, possible attacking vectors etc. On the other hand, these mistakes very rarely happen on the highest futsal level.

I want to you understand, that the **ball is important.** That is the fact. Ball is often the point of reference in defensive and attacking tactics. Especially important the position of the ball is in zonal system of defense, where the defensive formation in **90%** of cases is depending on where the ball is (and not, where opponent's player are). In individual cover it is also very important, where the opponent with the ball is located on the pitch and at what moment.

Nevertheless, regardless of how important the ball is, you should not be only thinking (and looking at) about where the ball is. Remember, that there are other factors too. Sometimes opponent will even try to make you concentrate on the ball instead of keeping an eye on players.

In this section of the book we will analyze situations, where a defender faces opponent without the ball. We will be learning to keep an eye on the ball and also (**simultaneously**) on your respective players (who at this moment are without the ball).

So it is easier for you, I decided to divide this chapter into 3 parts, where I will be talking at first about high pressure (defending team is positioned up the pitch, on opponent's half), defense in the middle of the pitch and also - inside our own half, on the **"last line of defense".**

High pressure

Let's start then with the situation, where a defending team is high up the pitch (next scheme). In this case we have a personal cover tactic.

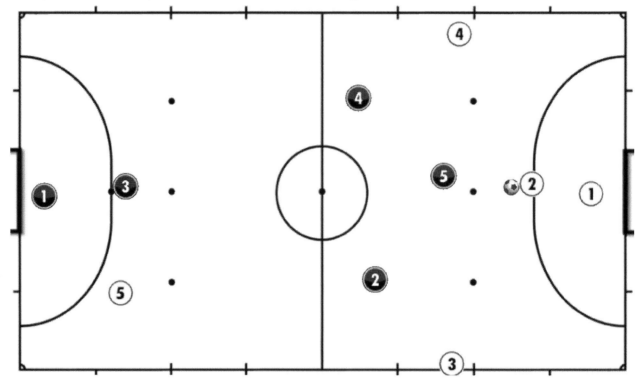

Let's take a closer look at how black team's player nr.2 should be defending. His priority is to cover the white player nr.3. There are different way to go about it, though.

The most popular mistake in this case (has to be said, that on the highest level these kind of mistakes happen rarely, mostly - in amateur or youth futsal) is that black nr.2 concentrates his attention on something one - either it's white nr.2 or white nr.3.

Here is what happens, if black nr.2 gives most of his attention to white nr.2 (player with the ball):

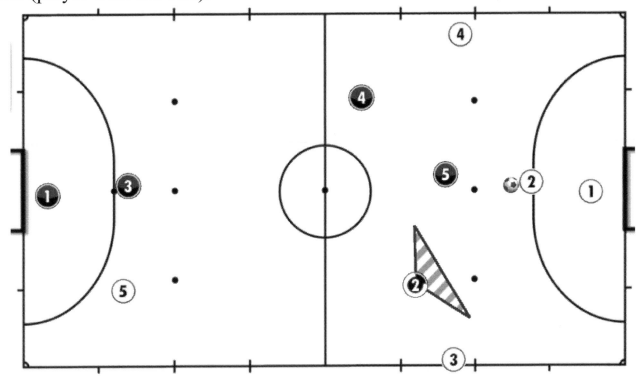

In this case (scheme above) black nr.2 is turned towards white nr.2. This causes **two problems**. First of all he loses the control of white nr.3. Second - he loses control of the central zone (middle of the pitch). This gives opponent an opportunity to use several vectors of attack (next scheme).

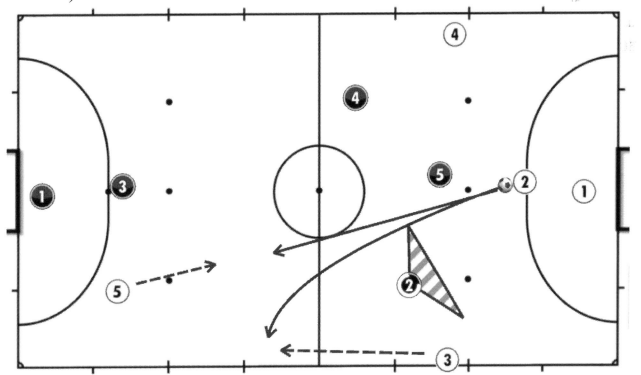

Black nr.2 should never forget that **regardless** of the defensive tactic, his team chooses (zonal, personal, switching or mixed), it's not only a player, we cover, who is the most important. We also have to understand the importance of controlling zones, where attack might be developing. When it's forgotten, it may lead to the following situations (next scheme):

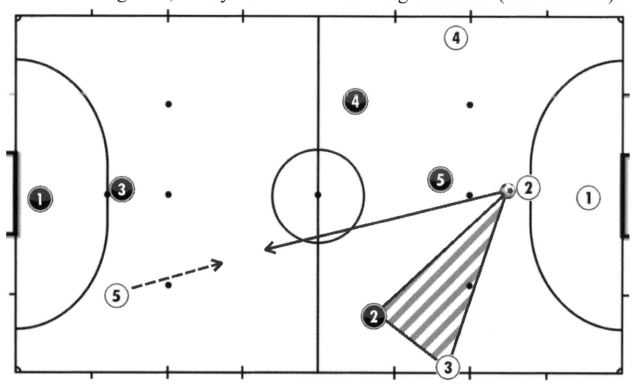

We can see, that black nr.2 used his peripheral vision (he sees simultaneously both the player with the ball and the player, who he is covering). Black nr.2 also positioned himself in a way, that he has time to react to any movement of white nr.3. So, what's the problem, then?

The problem is that black nr.2 **totally ignored the vector of attack**, which is shown on the previous scheme. That is - through the middle. This problem emerges from a player's brain - from his thinking. Also - from the lack of knowledge. So my job here is to give you knowledge and your's - to implement it in a game. Amateur futsal players often think, that since this is a personal cover - a job of a defender is to take his respective opponent and stay with him no matter what, not allowing his to take active part in attack. It's not exactly, how it should be done.

Yes, as a defender you should be covering your respective player. On the other hand you should never forget, that each defender's actions contribute to overall team (collective) defensive effort. Remember this, **futsal is not** a game of four separate players and a keeper against four separate players and a keeper. **Futsal is** a game or **team** of four players and a keeper against a team of four players and a keeper. Even if it's a personal cover, defensively you should be a **unit** of four players and a keeper!

This is the moment, I was leading you to. The moment, when we have to stop and learn one of the key concepts (defensive concepts, at least) of futsal - concept of **space orientation**.

If I had to give you a short **definition** of this concept, I would say, that **space orientation (in defense)** - it's an ability of a futsal player to take a certain position on the pitch, which will allow him to control potentially dangerous actions of a certain opponent's player and at the same time - potentially dangerous zones of opponent's team (collective) attack.

Let's take a look at some examples. If defensive player nr.2 is applying a concept of space orientation, he should take the following position (next scheme):

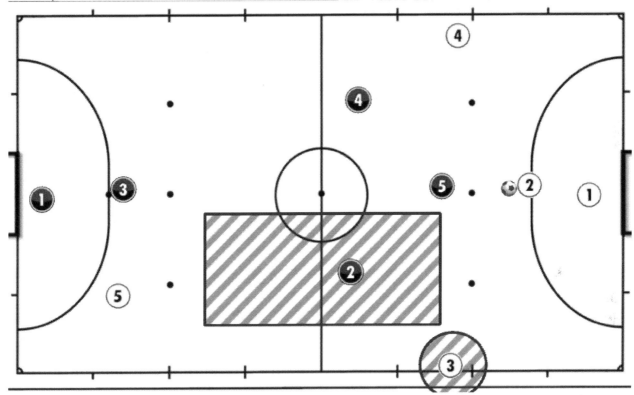

On the scheme above we can see, that black nr.2 took a position, where he simultaneously controls his respective opponent (white nr.3) and at the same time helps his team to control the middle part of the pitch. As a result of this positioning, black team stays compact as a defensive unit.

futsalicodvd.com | Youtube.com/futsalico_ENG | instagram@futsalico_ENG

Defense at the middle line of the pitch

We are going to take a look at the situation, where an active defending starts from the middle of the pitch. Let's start with a **correct** positioning of a defending team. This is a zonal defensive system:

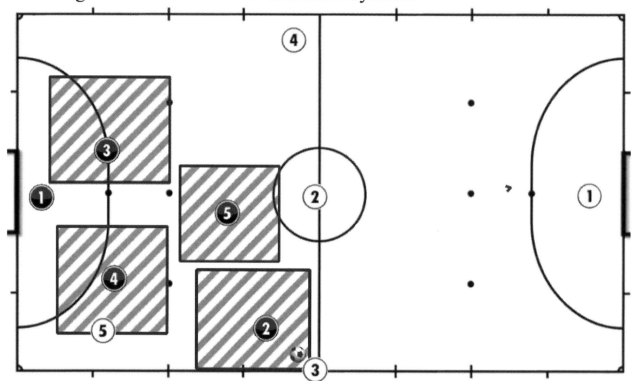

On the scheme above we can see, that all dangerous zones are controlled by a defending team.

Next scheme will show you a positioning of a defending team in the case of **personal cover** tactics:

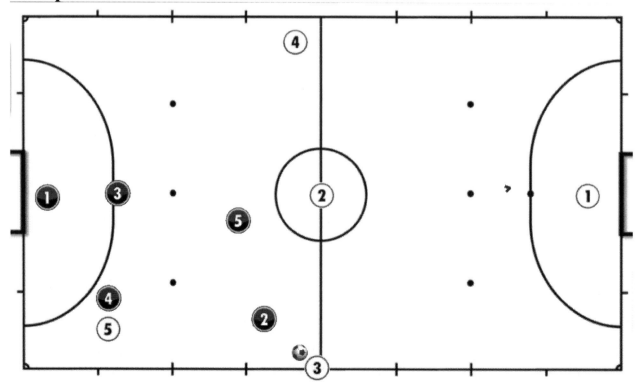

futsalicodvd.com | Youtube.com/futsalico_ENG | instagram@futsalico_ENG

On the scheme above you can see, that a black team is using a personal cover to take control of each player of an opponent. Now, attention - this is **incorrect** positioning!

The main mistake here is that two players of a black team positioned themselves, only thinking about their respective opponents. At the same time they **totally neglected space orientation concept**. I remind you, that space orientation concept would tell us to take such positions, where we could also contribute to collective defensive effort by controlling **dangerous zones**. **Can you find** two black players, who positioned themselves incorrectly?

In the next scheme I will show you zones, which are controlled by each player and respective opponents, which they are "taking":

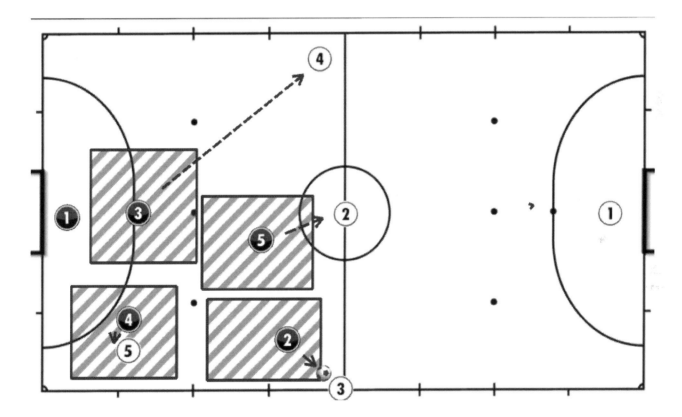

At first glance it looks like everything is correct. Defense is pretty solid, no real free spaces. Each player is controlled. Remember, I told you previously, that this is a **personal cover tactic** (type of defense is "personal cover"). This means, that while the ball moves, defensive players will also be moving in a certain way. Not, like they would be moving, for example, in zonal defense.

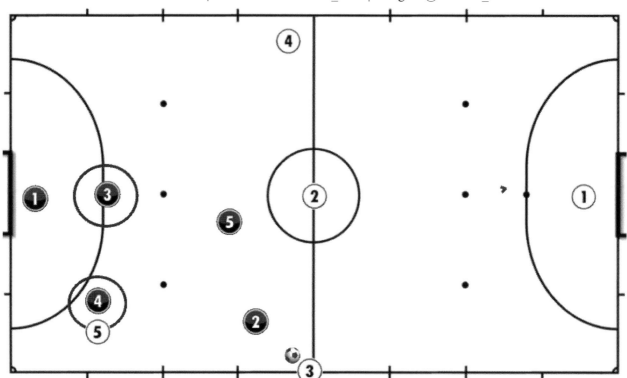

Two players of a black team are positioned incorrectly - black nr.4 and black nr.3. First of all, black nr.4 is positioned way too close to white nr.5. This will not allow him to anticipate opponent's movements. Black nr.4 is also positioned too wide (too far from the center). These two factors (being too close to his opponent and space behind the back of black nr.4) create potential danger and therefore - make team (collective) defense weaker.

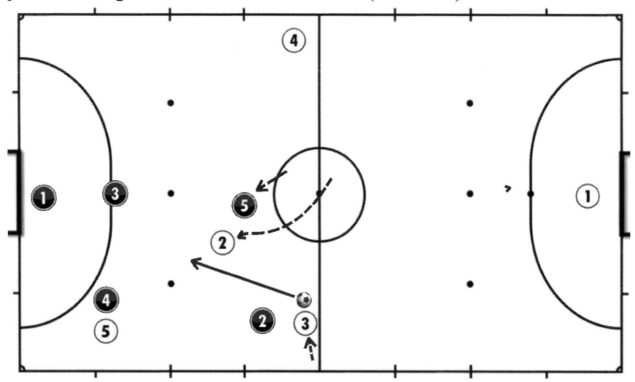

From this position, black nr.4 won't be able to help his partners in case they are outplayed and lose their respective opponents (scheme above).

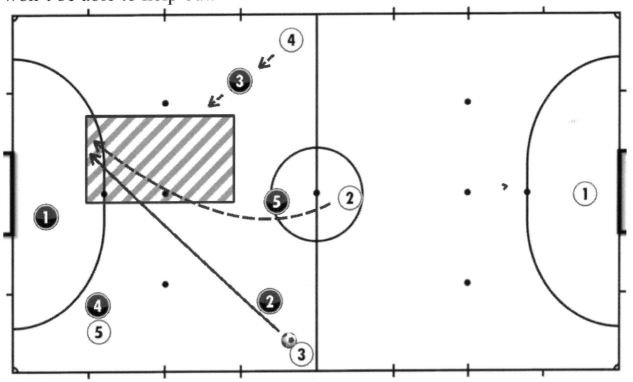

White nr.3 can outplay black nr.2 (scheme above). In this case black nr.4 won't be able to help out.

On the scheme above we can see, that black nr.3 took the correct position against his respective player (white nr.4) - he is 2-3m away, facing a player and can now make a controlled retreat with the low risk of being outplayed. On the other had, if he does get outplayed, non of his partners will be able to help. This is a result of the fact, that black nr.4 is positioned too wide on the flank. This creates big free space in the center of defensive formation.

Later I will show you the correct positioning of both black nr.4 and black nr.3. Before I do it, though, let's take a look at another case, where black nr.3 would be in **incorrect position**.

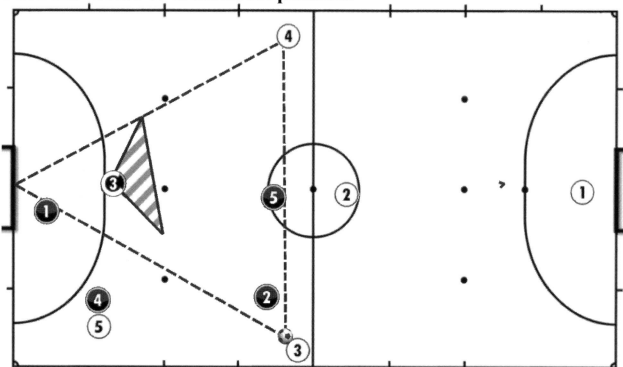

On the scheme above we can see, that black nr.3 took a position, which can be called as another **extreme**. In this case, black nr.3 formally made a lot of things correctly. That is - taking his position in a defensive triangle, turning his body correctly, using his peripheral vision (sees the ball and his respective player at the same time). So what is wrong with this position?

The main problem is that, when using personal cover tactic, black nr.3, should not forget, that he should be covering his respective player. On the scheme above we can see, that he controls dangerous zone, but totally neglects "his" opponent (white nr.4). White player nr.4 can easily take the ball, has time to get full control of it (make several touches), has time to gain speed.

In the case, if black nr.3 only stays in the zone, but allows white nr.4 so much time and space, then attacking player will be entering this zone already with a good control of the ball, high speed, clear plan therefore - with a huge advantage already. It will be very difficult for black nr.3 to stop his opponent.

So you can see, that neglecting one danger (for example - respective player) immediately means the other aspect (for example - zone) will be in danger too. Always take a position, which will allow you to control two aspects - your respective opponent and a potentially dangerous zone.

How can black nr.3 position himself in a way, which will allow to control white nr.4 and also assure the compactness of the zone behind defender's back? Next scheme will show you the best way, how black nr.3 can position himself:

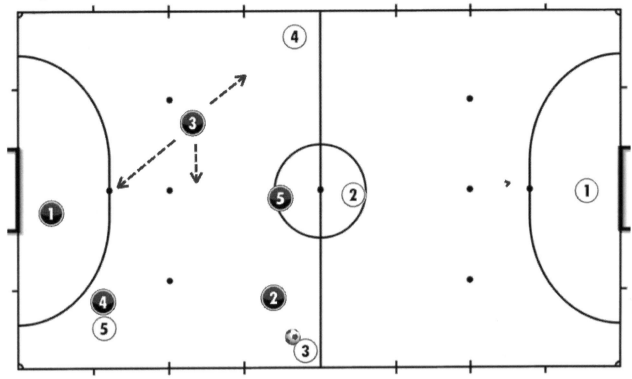

We can see (scheme above), that black nr.3 can reduce the distance to white nr.4 at any moment (if he receives the ball, for example). This will allow to contain opponent's advancing.

From this position black nr.3 is also able to support black nr.5. Black nr.3 can also get back (closer to his goal) in case, if black nr.2 is outplayed or in case if black nr.4 loses his respective player (white nr.5). This is a good example of an optimal position, which shows **a very good space orientation** by a black nr.3.

futsalicodvd.com | Youtube.com/futsalico_ENG | instagram@futsalico_ENG

On the next scheme you can see, which is the best positioning of all four field players of a black team:

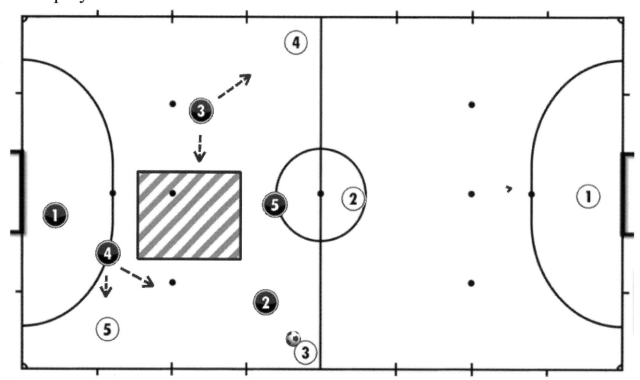

We can see the positioning of defensive players in a personal cover tactic, when space orientation concept is taken into consideration (all players and all potentially dangerous vectors of attack are controlled) - each player is taken and if any defending player gets outplayed, there would always be a teammate, who can support him.

futsalicodvd.com | Youtube.com/futsalico_ENG | instagram@futsalico_ENG

Defending close to your goal (last stand)

In this section we are going to take a look at the example, which will allow you to understand the space orientation completely. Next scheme will show you the situation, where two black team's players are positioned incorrectly:

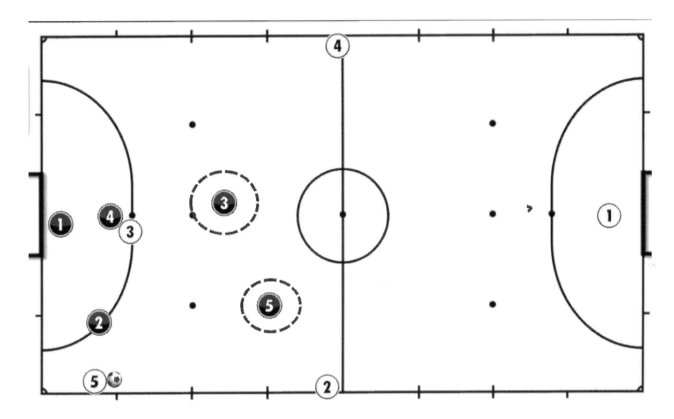

I guess you can already see, what is the mistake, which black nr.3 is making. He is too far away from his respective opponent (white nr.4). In zonal defensive tactic this positioning would not be ideal, but would still be allowed, then in personal cover it would be a huge mistake.

What do you think, black nr.5 is doing wrong? He is too far away from his goal. Let's see, how it can after the **collective defensive effort** and make a defensive structure weaker.

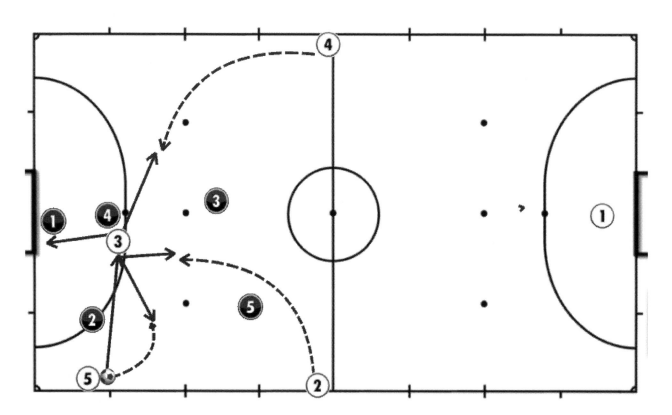

On the scheme above we can see, that in this particular situation (with black nr.5 being to advanced), the **biggest danger** for a defending team is the zone in-between black players. It gets even worse from a black team, because this space is already occupied by a white pivot!

If a pass goes to white nr.3, this will create a high risk of losing a goal. The main reason form that is that a pivot would be receiving the ball right in front of the goal! Any shot from this position for a decent pivot would almost definitely mean a goal. This situation is **dangerous** because there are different **options** for the **pivot**. If he doesn't shoot, he can play the ball to one of his partners, who can be taking a very dangerous first-touch shot.

What is the correct positioning for a defending team, then?

Let's take a look at the next scheme:

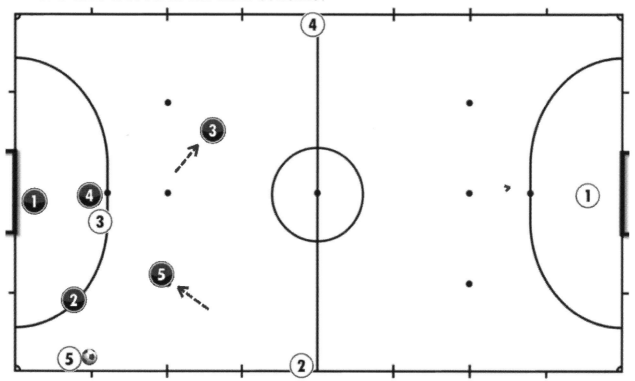

Black nr.3 moves closer to white nr.4 and this allows him to adequately react to any of his attacking movements. Black nr.5 in this case allows bigger distance to white nr.2. This would create a space for white nr.2, but the biggest danger right now comes from the pass to the middle. Therefore black nr.5 should take such position, so white nr.5 would not want to make a pass to the middle (and instead - would favor the pass to white nr.2).

White nr.5 should be realizing the danger of losing the ball in this position. This would create a very dangerous counter-attack by the black team, because all white players are on opponent's half. This is what black team is "playing on" - covering the **biggest risk** and makes opponent chose the vector of attack, which is less dangerous for a defending team.

Black nr.5 should not be getting too close to the middle though. It is enough to take a position, where a pass from white nr.5 to white nr.3 becomes unsafe (dangerous) for an attacking team.

DEFENSIVE TEAMPLAY

I spent some time thinking, whether I should include this topic in a book. I had an idea at first to talk about teamplay in the book, where I would concentrate on link-up play of groups of 2, 3 and 4 players. The topic "defensive teamplay" also needs to be talk about in terms of mistakes, which teams a often making. Mistakes is another topic I prefer to leave for series of books "Stupid futsal mistakes".

Later I understood, though, that since we spend much time on space orientation, we simple have to talk about defensive teamplay in this book. What I mean by this term - **defensive teamplay**? This is a sum of individual, but at the same time - well-coordinated defensive decisions and actions.

When I say "well-coordinated", I mean that each player is making his decisions, based not only on where the ball and opponents are, but also - where his teammates are (what they are doing, who they cover, what's their position etc.).

Let's move on to the first example.

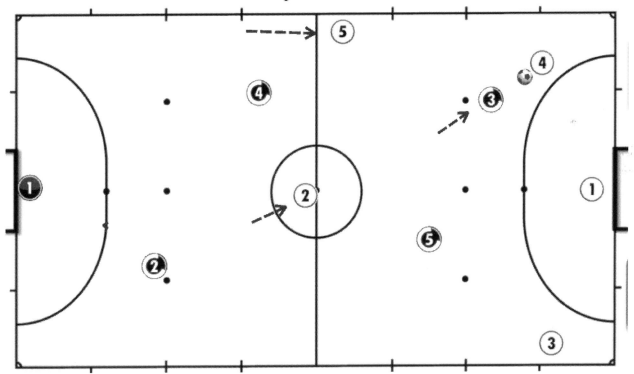

On the scheme above we can see, that black team is defending in a high pressing (3/4 of the pitch). White nr.4 experiencing some trouble with controlling the ball - didn't have a good first touch, so has to use several touches instead.

Black nr.3 sees this and decides to put some additional pressure and try to get the ball away from an opponent. Other opponent's players can see, that white nr.4 is in trouble and try to help him out. White nr.5 gets back down the flank, but white nr.2 gets towards the middle circle.

Usually in such situations those defending players, who are closer to their goal (at this moment in this example it's black nr.2 and black nr.4) are staying on their respective places. They often cannot read the situation and act accordingly. They do not adjust their positioning. This is a mistake.

The reason for this mistake is often a misconception of what compact defense means. They think, that the closer they are to their goal, the better it is for a defending side, the more compact and reliable the defensive structure is. Often defending players think, that the most important in to get back (closer to their goal) in time. They are wrong. **Often to make the defense more solid, you have to move up the pitch** (forward)!

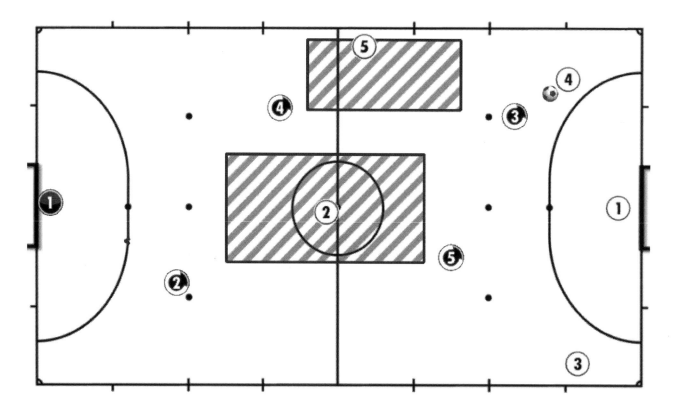

The scheme above shows us the space, which becomes free and gets out of control of the defensive team. Defensive structure is spread and becomes vulnerable. This happened, because black nr.2 and black nr.4 did not go up the pitch and did not put pressure to their respective players.

There is a simple rule, you have to remember. If your teammate is **successfully** pressuring an opponent with the ball, all defensive players have to apply pressure to their respective players **immediately**.

Scheme above shows us, what can happen, if black nr.2 and black nr.4 do not move forward in time. White nr.4 can play the pass to the flank, then the ball goes to the middle (to white nr.2). White nr.2 is not pressured by anyone. Black nr.2 had to be in the middle and immediately apply pressure on white nr.2. This did not happen, so white nr.2 has all the time in the world to get the ball under control, face our goal and even gain speed.

This situation will also mean a numeric advantage on white team - 3v2. All attacking player have a lot of space and time. Nightmare for defense. How should black nr.2 and black nr.4 deal with this now? They thought, that staying at the back (closer to their goal) would make their defense more solid. Instead we have a completely lost situation for a black team. In last two defenders move forward now, they risk to be outplayed on the counter movement. To keep staying at the back is not a good option too, because when white team's players gain some speed, they will easily outplay anyone. Without faints and dribbles. If black players try to tackle fast-going opponents, there is a high possibility, that there will be a fault.

Let's now see, what could have happened, if black nr.2 and nr.4 remembered about the space orientation concept and could read a game well (next scheme):

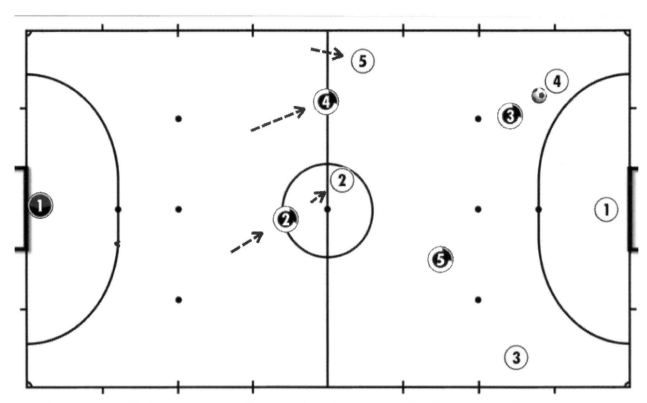

They would just move forward, closer to their respective opponents. That would allow to block the middle section of the pitch (no free spaces, no big distance between the lines of players - **compactness** all over the place).

Two things to remember, when moving forward like this, though. First of all, as I said previously - do not move until you are sure, that opponent's player with the ball is well pressured.

If black nr.3, for example, goes to pressure white nr.4 and gets outplayed, then all other defensive players would be acting a bit differently (there is another book of mine, where you can find explanation of defensive adjustments in case if one player is outplayed, so let's not waste our time and focus now). So before you move from your positions, make sure, that white nr.4 is really having trouble and black nr.3 has advantage in the fight for the ball there.

Second thing black nr.2, 4 and 5 have to remember is that, they should not move too close to their respective players. Do not move closer than 2 meters to them. Leave yourself some time and space to react to whatever your opponent has in mind. 2-3m distance to your respective opponents will still get them under pressure and will still allow you to stay compact as a team.

If you move from your positions before you make sure, that white nr.4 is under pressure and black nr.3 has an upper hand there in the fight for the ball, you can end up in a numeric disadvantage.

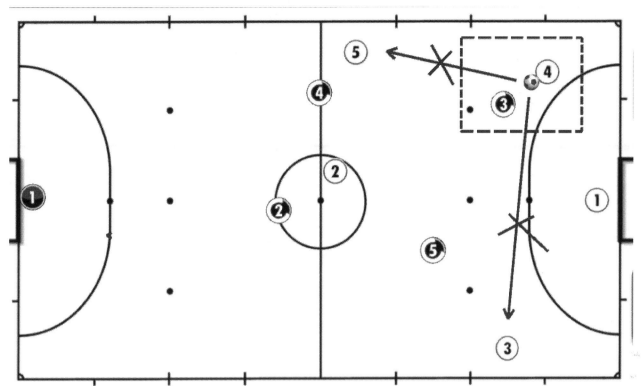

On the scheme above you can see the final result of a good defensive work by each player of a black team. White nr.4 is under pressure. He has two options for the pass and each of these options is risky, because the pass can be intercepted or the receiver of the pass (in our case it's white nr.3 and white nr.5) can immediately get under severe pressure and still lose the ball. Giving the fact, that white nr.4 is under pressure, he will probably have trouble making an accurate pass. This will also go in favor of a defending team.

White nr.4 can try to outplay black nr.3, but giving the fact that he is well-pressured and that black nr.3 is not jumping forward (but instead - pressures smartly and bit-by-bit), that would be a very risky move by white nr.4. Player with the ball should also not forget, that he is the last player. Any mistake in that area would mean almost a certain goal.

Most probably this situation will end with defensive team getting the ball away from white team or with a corner-kick or a kick-in. I am not saying, that it's guaranteed, that black team will be getting the ball away from their opponents. I am saying, that the chances of this happening are very high.

Now you can see, how one well-timed adjustment of positioning can lead to completely different game situation.

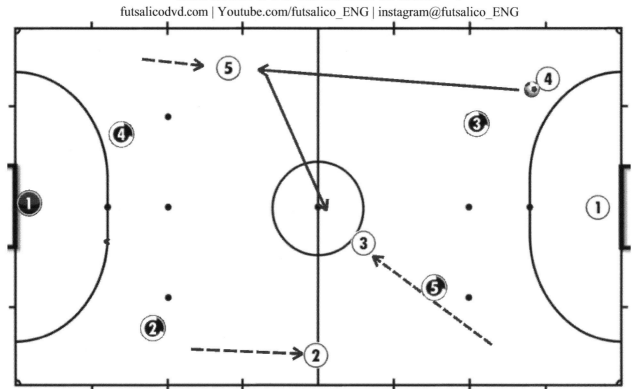

Here is another example (scheme above) of ignoring space orientation. This time it's so very popular amongst amateurs formation 2-2. Black nr.3 applies pressure on white nr.4. Black nr.2 and black nr.4 are late to adjust their positions. As a **result** we have 3v2 situation with white team having so much time and space.

Try to remember about space orientation, whichever defensive strategy or formation you choose. This will save you load of points and will allow you to stay in the fight for medals in the tournament.

SPACE ORIENTATION TRAINING

This section is about getting your team ready for defensive play, which involves keeping an eye on respective opponent's players, while simultaneously applying space orientation.

Here is a drill, for which you need 1/2 of the pitch. This is a futsal game, which includes frequent one on one **defensive duels**. These duels teach players to use personal cover on a regular basis and at the same time - know where teammates are and what situation they are in.

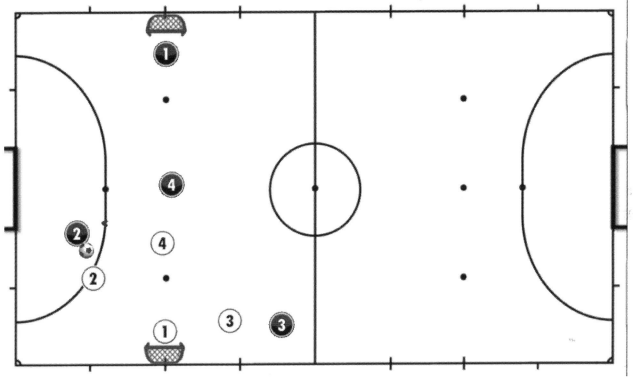

Set-up: 3 field players and one goalie (can play 3v3 without goalkeepers) in each team

Equipment: 2 pair of goals (better if these are small floorball goals) - smaller than futsal goals. But if you don't have such goals - use which ever pair of goals you have.

Intensity: high

Duration: 2 halves of 10 minutes each. Playing for result - to make players more motivated. Losers of each 10 minute game make 30 push-ups.

Conditions: Each player always plays only against a certain player in opponent's team. In our case, for example, it's black nr.2 against white nr.2, black nr.3 against white nr.3 and black nr.4 against white nr.2. Always. Black nr.2, for example, can never tackle or intercept a pass, made by anyone, but his respective white nr.2. So if white nr.3 passes the ball, only black nr.3 can intercept this pass. If white nr.4 has a ball, only black nr.4 can tackle him etc.

You can use t-shirt of similar colour in each team. For example, one team would consist on 1 red, 1 blue and 1 white t-shirt. Same colours have to be in another team. Only players, wearing t-shirts of similar colour could play against each other.

This drill can be used simultaneously on both parts of the pitch. Depending on the amount of players on the training session, you can play 3v3, 4v4 or even 5v5 on each half.

It is very important to keep the drill **dynamic**, so players are not waiting for their turn to play for too long. Try to think your training session through and plan it in a way, so there is no long breaks between drills and also inside drills.

You can be playing a regular game of futsal (without a necessity to play against a certain player). You can play 3v3, 4v4, 5v5. With or without keepers. You should remember, though, that you should tell your players, what is the objective of the training session. What they should be focusing on while playing.

First of all, gather players around you and tell them, that space orientation while defending is the main objective of this drill. Use a tactics board to explain them the main concept. Then show them their positioning in certain cases.

While players are completing the drill (playing a game), the job of the coach is to observe and detect mistakes. If there is a mistake, which is worth explaining and correcting, the play should be stopped. Players have to remain, where they are. Coach (captain or coach-player) enters the pitch and shows, where the mistake is and how it should be done correctly.

This kind of explanation is not just for those, who made a mistake. It's also for the rest of the guys. So they have to pay attention. This is also the time and place for asking questions. Let players engage in the discussion and make them suggest possible salvation of the problem.

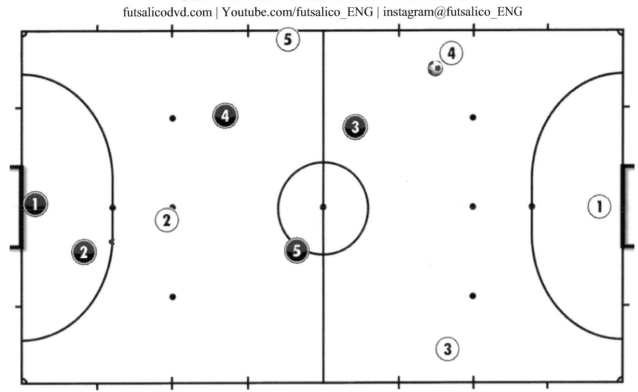

Make sure you eventually pass on the knowledge, which players gained during the drill, to real futsal training match (on the full pitch). The main objective of any drill and to teach and create a correct habit. The objective of a training futsal match is to test the knowledge and see, if **habits** are not forgotten, when stress and tiredness comes into place. Therefore make sure, that players understood the idea and started to gain correct habits, before moving to a full pitch match.

I would say, that ideally, a training session should consist of one warm-up drill, one or two main drills and only then - a full pitch training match. Remember, that each drill should have the same single objective!

Why you should be using 1/2 of the pitch in your drills? There is another book, where I give full detailed explanation of the ways to create training plans and create and implement futsal drills (available on futsalicodvd.com). Therefore I am not going to dive into small details here. Still I would like to explain the main idea, what 1/2 pitch drills are for.

Such drills give players an opportunity to encounter certain game situations more frequently. If an objective of the drill is teaching players to defend in 1v1 situations, that means, that amount of such situations during, say, 10 minutes will be bigger on the half of the pitch, then on the full pitch. When playing only on one half of the pitch, futsalers will have less time and space. Therefore, will be under bigger pressure. That means, that it is going to be a bit easier for them, when they play on the full pitch. It doesn't mean, though, that each and every drill should be performed on the half of the pitch.

OPPONENT IS ABOUT TO RECEIVE THE BALL

MAIN PRINCIPLES

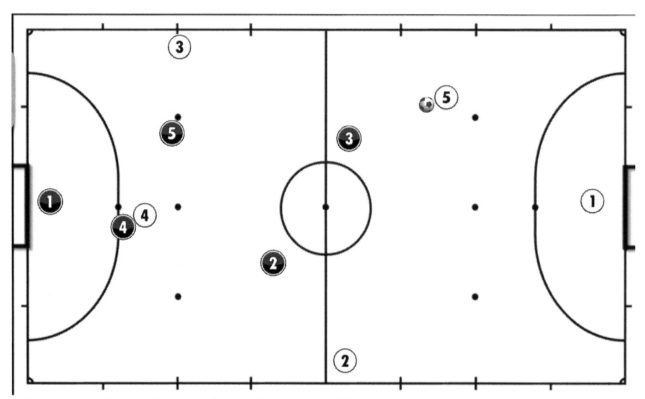

Let's analyze, how a defender should be playing. We are going to use a situation, which is shown on the scheme above. Our main **focus** is on the actions of black nr.5.

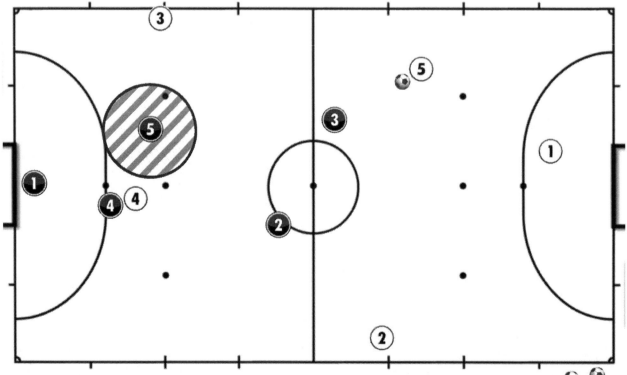

First of all, the positioning of this player has to allow him to see both his opponent (white nr.3) and the ball. At the same time he should try to locate himself on the pitch in a way, so he can gather information from the pitch - (read the game). For example, he has to know, where are his teammates and opponents.

I am not saying, that he has to see them non-stop - each and every moment. I am saying, that his **positioning** should allow him to orientate himself against other players and that is only possible if a slight turn of his head gives him an opportunity to see any area of the pitch.

His location on the pitch is not enough to achieve that. It is achievable if he doesn't concentrate (turns to) only on the ball or only on his respective player. Peripheral vision might come in handy in this case.

Black nr.5 should also position himself, so he can help black nr.3 in case if white nr.5 outplays him.

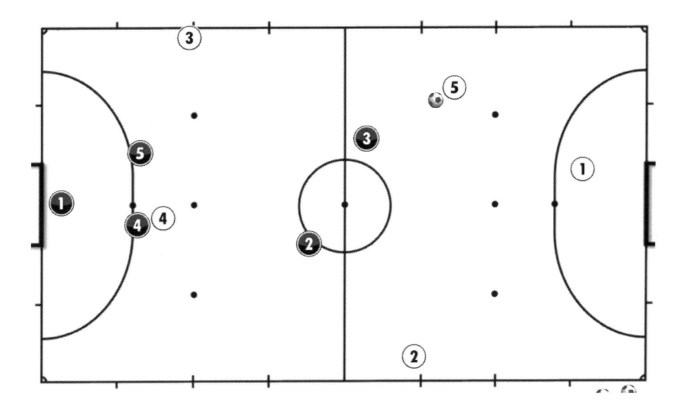

Scheme above shows us the example of positioning by black nr.5, where he can see both white nr.3 and the ball. Which seems to be correct. On the other hand, black nr.5 cannot support black nr.3 from this position.

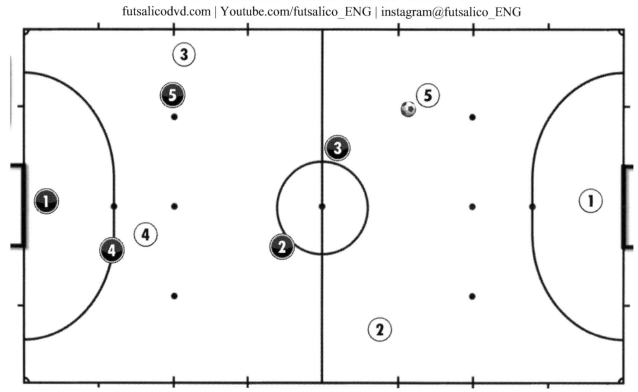

Here is another example, where black nr.5 formally (on paper) is positioned correctly, but in reality this position is very wrong. Black nr.5 uses peripheral vision from this position and is able to see simultaneously white nr.3 and also - the player with the ball (white nr.5). The positioning of black nr.5 doesn't allow him to help his partner (black nr.3) in case, if white nr.5 goes past him. Black nr.5 also leave the zone behind the back of black nr.3 too wide open. This creates serious weakness in overall team **defensive structure**.

You can see now, that a defender has to take many different game aspects into consideration, when he chooses his positioning. This is exactly, what I will try to teach you to do. First of all, you have to get knowledge and then uses drills to create playing habits. Let us move on now to those situations, when our respective opponent (the player, who we are covering) is about to receive the ball.

BALL IS ON IT'S WAY TO YOUR OPPONENT

This is a section, where we will be talking about situations, when our respective opponent is about to receive the ball. That would mean, that the ball is already traveling to opponent's player, but he is yet to receive it.

We will be concentrating on what a defender should be doing in this case. What are his possible actions and **consequences**. We will also take a look at some mistakes defenders often make in this type of situations.

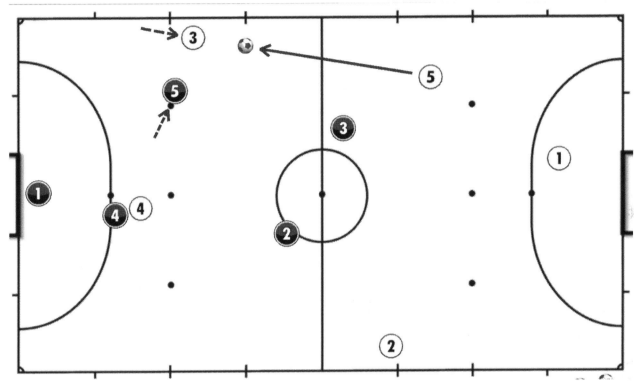

Take a look a the scheme above. White nr.5 just made a pass. As soon as the pass is made, player nr.5 of a black team (defender) starts his movement towards his respective opponent (white nr.3). So the first thing to do is to make this first step forward. Then a defender has to make up his mind - what to do next. He has to think fast, so it's not always easy, but the more tactical knowledge you have, the more your train and gain experience in games, the faster and more rational your decisions will be.

Here are **possible scenarios** in this situation:

1. **Defender can allow** white nr.3 to receive the ball. In this case defender just stops 1.5-2m away from his respective opponent.

2. **Defender can attack the passing lin**e (from white nr.5 to white nr.3) and interceps the pass.

In case if the ball goes fast accurately and black nr.5 cannot make it in time to interceps such pass (or he is not sure, that he can be beat white nr.3 in the sprint for the ball), defender should not try to intercept!

This is a very important moment, because if a defender doesn't get to the ball faster, than his opponent, there is a high risk, that a defender might lose the control of his opponent. This would allow white nr.3 to got into a free space behind the back of a defender and would create a very dangerous situation (scheme below).

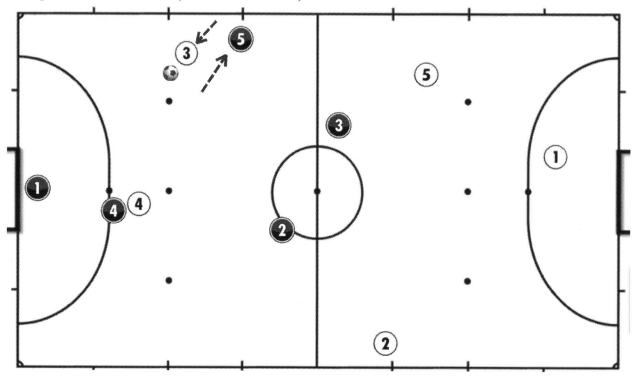

Here is **correct positioning** in case, if the pass was strong and accurate:

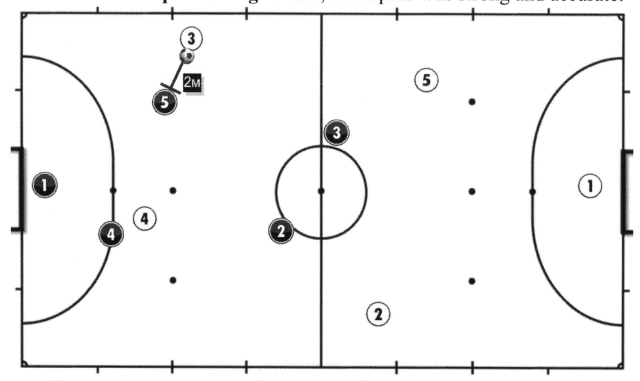

As you can see on the scheme above, a defender took in position 1.5-2m from his respective opponent. Now it's time to evaluate, how opponent received the ball.

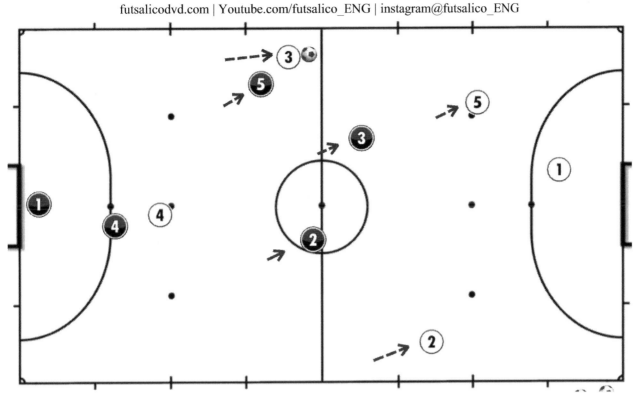

If an opponent didn't receive the ball well (for example, his first touch was bad and now he needs another couple of touches to take the ball under control), a defender should use this opportunity to pressure his opponent. If pressure is timed and applied well, defender might end-up turning his opponent towards his goal (as shown on the scheme above).

This will give a defender initiative and control over the situation. All defending players must read this situation and get closer to their respective opponents and put all possible lines under pressure. This might lead to a situation, when white nr.3 won't have any safe passing option anymore and won't have any other choice other than keep the ball and shield it. This would be a good moment for black nr.5 to get into aggressive pressure and try to get the ball away from white nr.3. It's important to do it without fouling, of course.

In the next scheme we are going to take a look at the situation, where white nr.3 managed to receive the ball very well (with the first touch) and got it under control immediately.

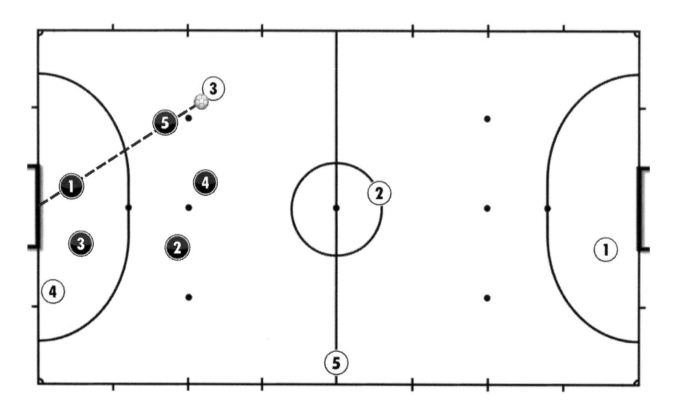

If that happens, black nr.5 should stay on the distance of 2m and contain the player with the ball. If white nr.3 moves forward, black nr.5 also moves towards his goal, but always keeps the distance of 2m. The ideal position for a defender would be on the imaginary lines between the ball and the center of the goal:

WHEN AND HOW TO INTERCEPT

One of the biggest dilemma for a defender will always be deciding, when to intercept the ball and when - not to do it (allow some freedom for opponent and wait for his next move). This is exactly, what we are going to analyze in this section for the book. I will try to give you an answer, when and how you should engage in the fight for the ball (in this case I mean interception, not tackling).

One thing should be said immediately - **you have to intercept**, when you are sure, you will take the ball. I am not speaking about calculated decision only, because we can never know for 100%, whether we will take the ball in a certain tackle or not. Some risk is always there and if we do not take it from time to time, we might never intercept nothing.

What I want to get to you is, that before intercepting a ball (attacking the line of the pass) in certain situation, defender should have an inner confidence, that he **can** take this exact ball in this exact situation. Consider that to be a certain belief. Defender should believe, he can be faster to the ball, than his opponent, before even thinking to throw yourself towards the ball.

If you are not sure, that this is a correct moment or correct situation to intercept, **then do not do it!** In this case just take the waiting position (1.5-2m away), let opponent to receive the ball, block a dangerous zone and wait for an opponent to come at you. At least, when he does, you will be ready!

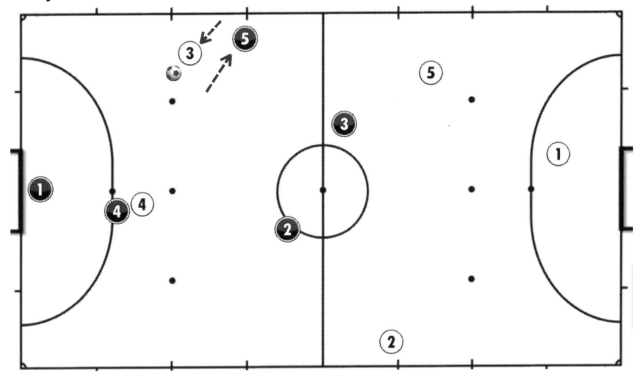

If you throw yourself into a interception in the situation, when you are not sure this is a good idea, there is a good chance you're going to lose the fight for the ball, lose your positioning and will easily be outplayed (scheme above).

If you are sure, you are going to make it to the ball first and win it - attack the passing line!

If you are not sure, that this is a right moment for you to engage - take defensive position, cover dangerous zones and wait.

Although this inner confidence is not an abstract term. It goes with the player and is always based on two factors: tactical knowledge (ability to read the game) and experience. These are two things you have to work on, if you want to become a better defender.

Your confidence will grow with your ability to read the game (know, how the game works and what are possible scenarios in certain situation) and also - with you expanding your limits. The more skillful, tactically equipped and experienced you are, the better you will be able to detect the right moment to try to intercept the ball.

There are **factors**, you have to take into a consideration before making a decision, whether you should intercept the pass or not:

1. **How strong was the pass**
2. **How accurate was the pass**
3. **How well-timed was the pass**
4. **How far a defender is from the line of the pass**
5. **How far an opponent is from the ball**
6. **What is the strongest foot of an opponent, who is about to receive the ball**
7. **Whether a defender has a cover (partner, who can help in case, defender is outplayed)**
8. **How fit and how skillful is an opponent, who is about to receive the ball**
9. **What is the score and time left in the match**
10. **Global tournament goals a team has.**

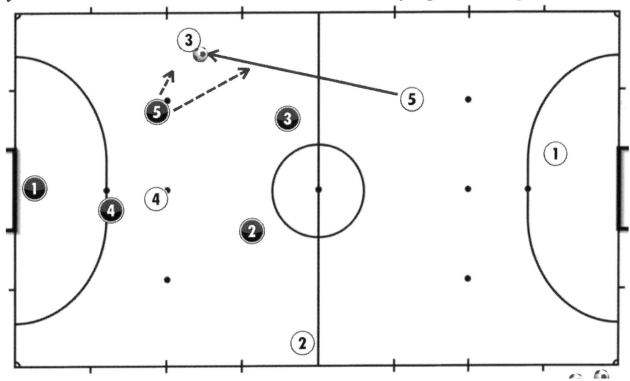

I would like to stress again - if your opponent (in this case white nr.3) is ready to receive the ball (means - he is open, concentrated, in correct positioning, can see his partner, asking for the ball etc.), then in most cases you should **let** him receive the ball instead of trying to intercept.

If the ball goes on opponent's strongest foot, but a defender is too far away from the passing line, then in most cases you a defender should let his opponent to receive the ball (scheme above).

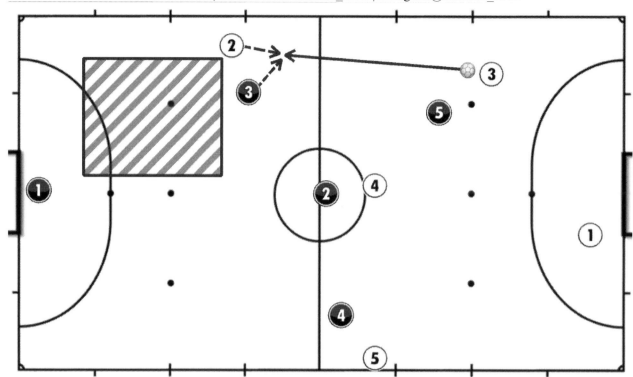

Here is a another case (scheme above), when you should think twice about intercepting. If the pass doesn't go with enough speed (which is good for a defender), opponent and defender are at the same distance to the ball (which is also good sign for a defender), but a defender doesn't have any backing-up from his teammates. There is a free space behind defender's back. In this case, a defender should in most cases choose an option to not attack the passing line.

If an attacking player beats defender to the ball, he might be going 1 on 1 with the keeper. I am sure, you will agree, that it's better to let opponent have the ball and then apply a controlled defense, then let opponent the chance to go up against your keeper.

Ok, enough of "when not to do it". Let's see, how situations, where a defender must try to intercept the ball, look like. This will give you better understanding and improve your decision-making skill.

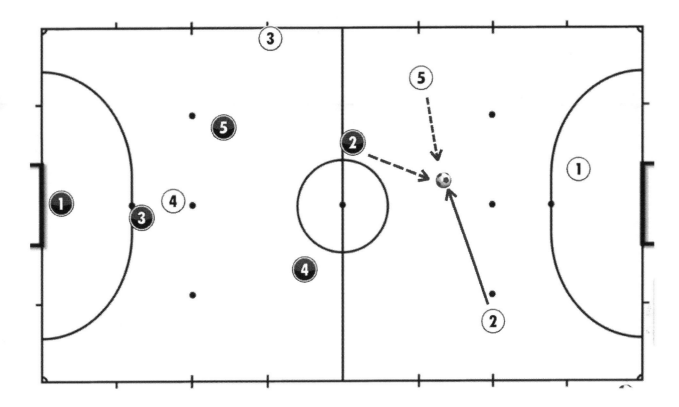

The scheme above gives you an example of a situation, where the distance from a defender (black nr.2) and his opponent (white nr.5) to the ball is the same. There is also a cover (black nr.4 or black nr.5) just in case. No free space behind black player's nr.2 back. Another argument in favor of intercepting is the fact, that the ball is on opponent's half and if black nr.2 intercepts this pass, he will immediately go one on one with the keeper.

This situation is perfect for intercepting. Although, you have to remember, that this **doesn't give you a 100% guarantee** of successful interception. On a professional level, for example, such a pass could go with high speed and perfect accuracy.

Sometimes (or even oftentimes) professional players (or amateur players of good quality) would just play at the back with pretentiously dangerous passes.

futsalicodvd.com | Youtube.com/futsalico_ENG | instagram@futsalico_ENG

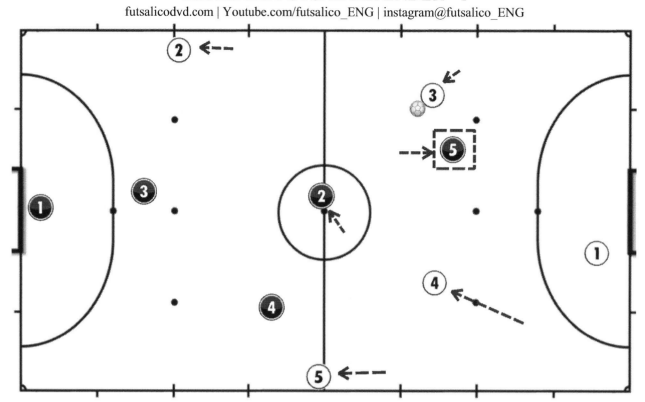

Their objective would be to lure defending team's player forward and make him attack passing lines. When he throws himself forward, they would just leave him behind and create a quick attack with a numeric advantage. You can see the result of this on the scheme above.

In every situation, where you have to make a decision whether to try intercept a pass or not, also take into consideration, what is the score at the moment, what time is left to the end of the game and what are your team's objectives in this game in terms of the tournament.

For example, if your team is ahead, there is not much time left in the game and you badly need three points, then isn't it better to form a controlled and compact defensive system and not risk too much? This might be obvious now, but, believe me, many players (especially amateurs or young) are not thinking about such things during the game. They see the ball, see the opportunity and they go for it. That is it. This leads to making unnecessary mistakes, lost points and as a result - the chances for medals in the tournament are gone.

There is also a factor of a game plan, which a coach (captain, coach-player etc.) sets for the team. Let's say a coach tells a team to player with maximum safety at the back and only get into interceptions in those situations, where the success of such play is almost assured. On the other hand, where situation is questionable, coach asks to take a defensive position and let an opponent get the ball.

If and when a futsal player has a certain understanding of all those factors (and their influence on a decision), we talked about previously, then such a player will always be more confident during the game. He (or she) won't be loosing much time and energy for a decision-making process.

Remember, though, that "There's a difference between knowing the path and walking the path" (told by Morpheus to Neo at the beginning of the cult movie "Matrix"). So knowledge and knowledge only is not enough. You have to gain match experience and also improve and perfect your skills on a training session (with the help of drills).

OPPONENT WITH THE BALL

POSITIONING ON THE PITCH

Let's start with player's positioning on the pitch. We have a situation, in which a defender faces opponent with the ball (next scheme):

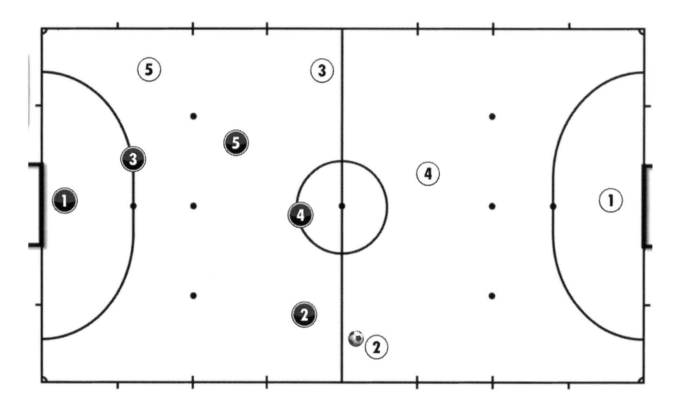

Black nr.2 is up against white nr.2. At this moment defending player is positioned correctly. When you (as a defender) make a decision, which is that point of the pitch, you are going to be placing yourself, you have to remember that the most important for you is to be **on the line between the ball and the center of the goal**. Also remember about the distance to your respective player: it has to vary from 1.5m and 2m.

There is another condition. You have to locate yourself in a imaginary triangle, which is formed by three dots:

1. Ball
2. Respective opponent
3. Center of your goal

futsalicodvd.com | Youtube.com/futsalico_ENG | instagram@futsalico_ENG

Next illustration shows us this **triangle** in regard to black nr.2:

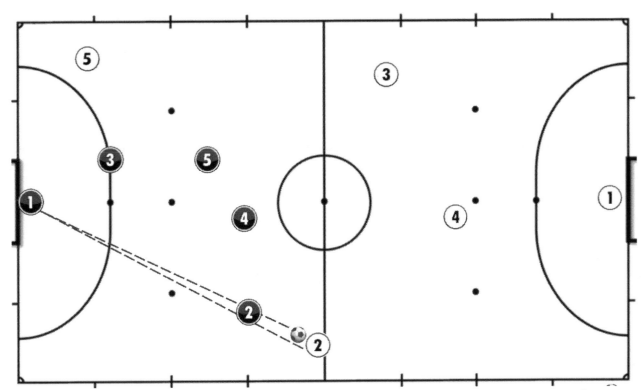

The same principle is applied to defending team's players, who are playing against opponents **without the ball**. For example, here is a triangle, of the black nr.3:

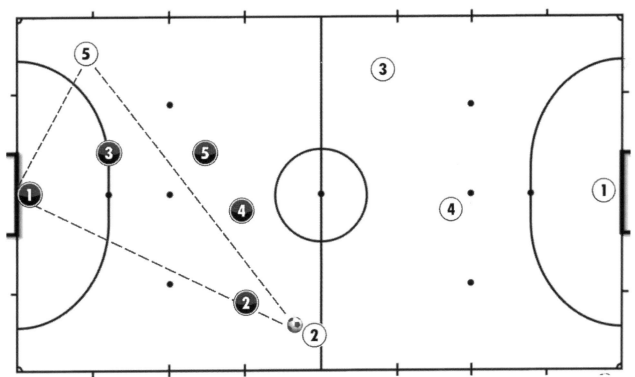

Scheme above shows you the correct positioning of a defending player nr.3.

Next schemes illustrate two example of **incorrect** positioning of black nr.3 (he is outside of the triangle):

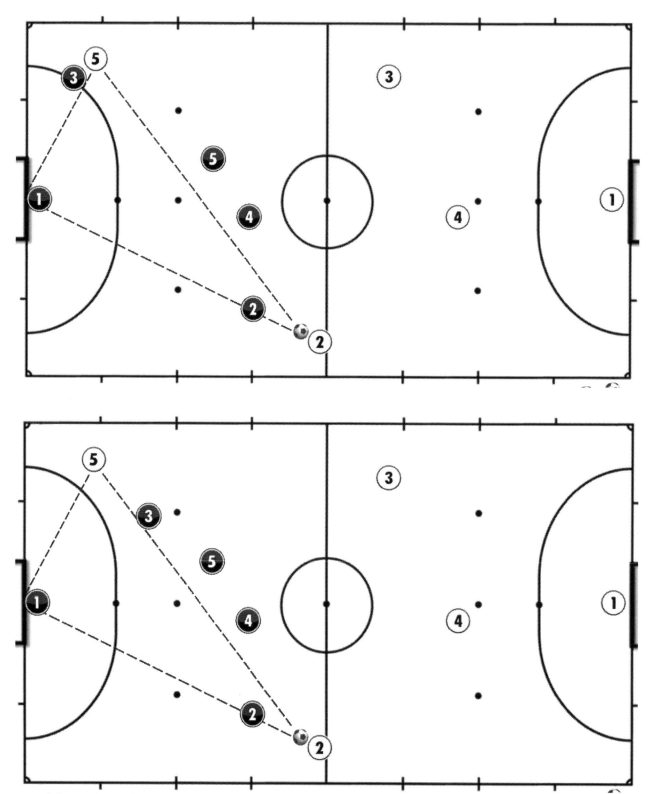

This triangle concept can be applied in regard to all pitch players. Regardless of who a defender is up against: opponent with the ball or without it.

HOW TO WIN THE BALL FROM OPPONENT

In this section we are talking about the body position (shoulders, sides, legs etc.) of a defender, who is up against an opponent with the ball. Here is an example of black nr.5 positioning:

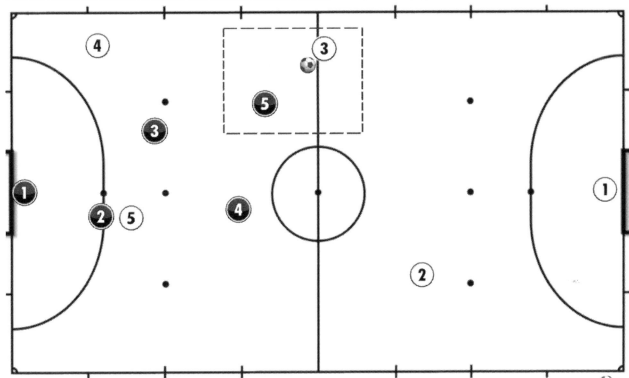

Defender in this case has face his opponent. Although, he should be standing at a slight angle: take one of his feet (and the same shoulder) a bit forward: right foot and right shoulder a bit forward or left foot and left shoulder a bit forward. **Here is an example of how it has to be done:**

futsalicodvd.com | Youtube.com/futsalico_ENG | instagram@futsalico_ENG

Next two pictures will show you an **example of how you should not** be standing against a player with the ball:

Both cases show you situations, where defenders will be easily losing their balance, if an opponent quickly changes the direction of his run.

HOW TO POSITION YOUR BODY

Black nr.5 is up against a white nr.3 on the left flank of the defense. If in this case, black nr.5 puts his left foot forward, then his weakest zone would be to his left (as next scheme shows):

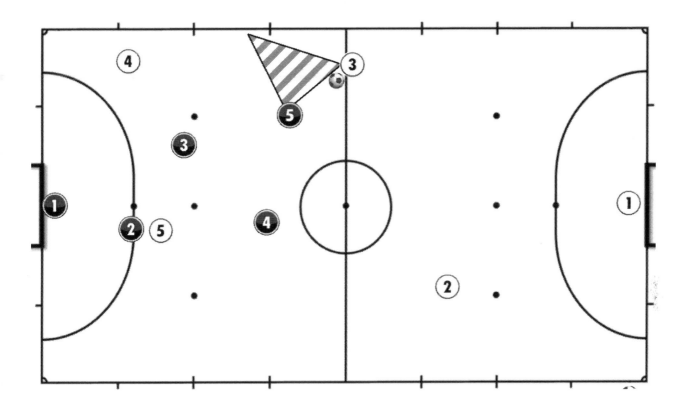

Black nr.5 would be much more interested for his opponent to go to another side (to black player's right). How black nr.5 can achieve that? He can take his left foot a bit forward and approach his opponent slightly from the left (from the side line). This would make white nr.3 think twice before going to his right (towards the flank) and he will most probably continue to his left (towards the center of the pitch):

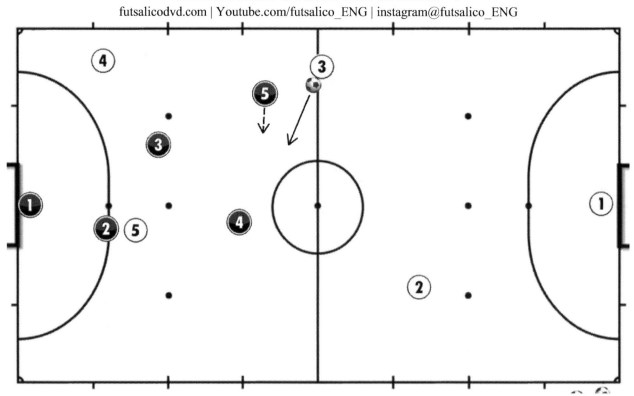

After a defender manages to get his opponent to the necessary direction, now it is time to start closing the distance (slowly and with a control) and if there is a good opportunity - tackle him to try and take the ball away.

SPACE ORIENTATION

We already talked about the importance of the position of the ball on the pitch and it's influence on defensive orientation and positioning of defenders. We talked about it mostly in the section "Opponent without the ball".

Space orientation may be different. The concept may change a bit as the status of your opponent (with or without the ball in his possession) changes. In this section of the book we will talk space orientation, when facing a player, who has the ball at his feet. I will introduce you to the main principles and we will also go through some most popular mistakes in this regard.

Here is a situation to **analyze**:

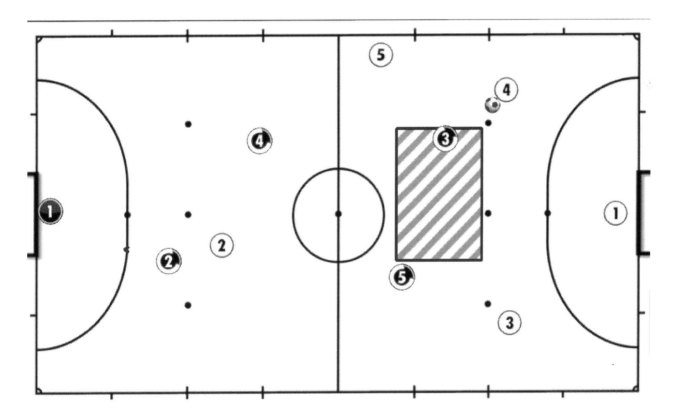

Black player nr.3 is up against the opponent with the ball (white nr.4). The main priority of a defender at this very moment is to cover his opponent. Although in order to be as much efficient as possible black nr.3 must understand, that he is a part of the defensive unit. It is like that regardless of the defensive tactic. So even in the case, when defending team chooses personal cover as their defensive approach, each and every player is still a part of whole defensive unit. That would mean, each and every defending player must take into a consideration, where his teammates are and how they are coping with their defensive duties. Applying space orientation means, that defenders remember, that they are the part of the team.

The previous scheme shows the territory, the space, which black nr.3 must always remember about. What does it mean? It means, he cannot throw himself on his opponent (trying to win the ball) without thinking. He must always evaluate, what are possible consequences of that. If he loses the fight for the ball, white team would have an advantage. That would mean, that all the rest of black team's players would have to provide support. In order to do that, they would have to readjust their positioning in order to compensate and restore compactness of defensive system.

Black nr.3 also has to remember, how he positions his body: which foot is in-front, which side he approaches his opponent from and why, what would be the best for and opponent to move etc. If I had to put it simple, I would say, that the **ideal position of a defender** would always be as high up the pitch (closer to opponents goal) as it is possible, but at the same time at the position, which allows to defend the space behind him in the best way possible.

Understanding the concept of space orientation is one of the most important jobs of any futsaler. This skill should be coached starting from at least age of 12 (if we are talking about kids). If these are adult amateur players, then - space orientation drills would have to be implemented ina training process right after they've improved most important futsal skills.

Let's get back to our example. Most problems of defenders begin after opponent, who has has ball, gives it away (passes it to this teammate).

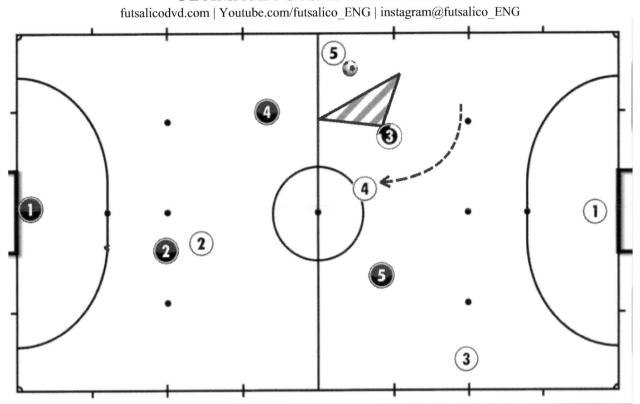

This would be the moment, when defending player tend to forget about space orientation (scheme above). He forgets, that no matter the status of his respective opponent (with or without the ball) a defender has to keep guarding the space behind himself. The situation, which is shown here is typical. Especially for youth and amateur players (especially for the beginners). After the pass is made to white nr.5, players, who are in position of black nr.3, very often tend to turn towards the ball, completely forgetting about their respective player and the space behind their backs.

If black nr.3 remembered about the concept of space orientation, he would play differently in this situation. These kinds of mistakes also happen, because the peripheral vision principle is ignored.

The thing is that these two concepts (**peripheral vision and space orientation**) are very similar in terms of their meaning and importance. Both these concepts have to be trained starting from the age of 12 (and in the first 2 years in futsal - for amateur adults). Both these concepts (or skills, if you will) are one of the most important ones, when it comes to a futsal defense. Both individual and team defense.

futsalicodvd.com | Youtube.com/futsalico_ENG | instagram@futsalico_ENG

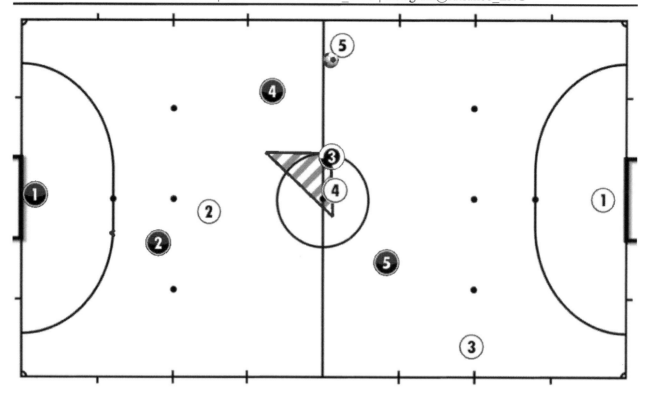

Here is another example (scheme above) of a defensive mistake by black nr.3. This time black nr.3 followed his respective opponent. This seams to be **correct** from the first look (defender follows and opponent and also is in the middle section of the pitch, which seems to allow the defensive system stay compact (no free space in the middle).

On the other hand the defender totally forgot about the principle of peripheral vision and completely lost the sight of the ball.

This happened for a couple of **reasons**. First would be too advanced (too high up the pitch) positioning on the pitch and too close to his respective player (white nr.4). This led to a defender not being able to react to the run of white nr.4 (defender did not have enough distance to his opponent to be able to react to whatever he was doing). Another reason would be that a defender forgot or didn't know about the principle of peripheral vision in futsal, which says that a defender should always simultaneously see his opponent and the player with the ball.

As a result, black nr.3 is located in the space, he has to defend, but at the same time has absolutely no influence on what is happening on the pitch. He doesn't contribute to team defense and cannot help his team much. Next scheme will show, what I mean:

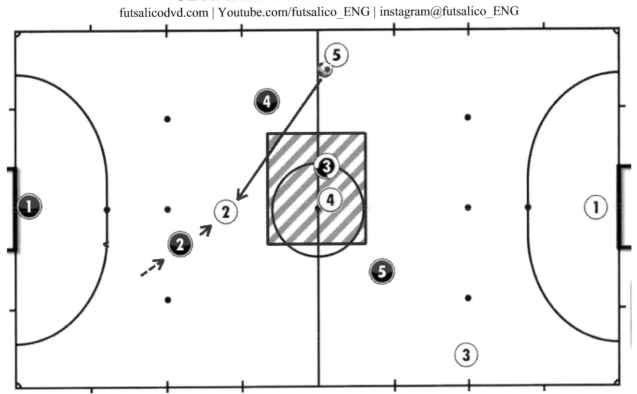

Scheme shows, that white nr.5 can easily pass to white nr.2 and the pass goes through the space, which should have been defended by black nr.3. If black nr.3 would use space orientation and peripheral vision principles to take his defensive position, he would not allow such a pass. Let's take a look at the next scheme and see, how black nr.3 should have played here in order to keep the center of the defensive system safe:

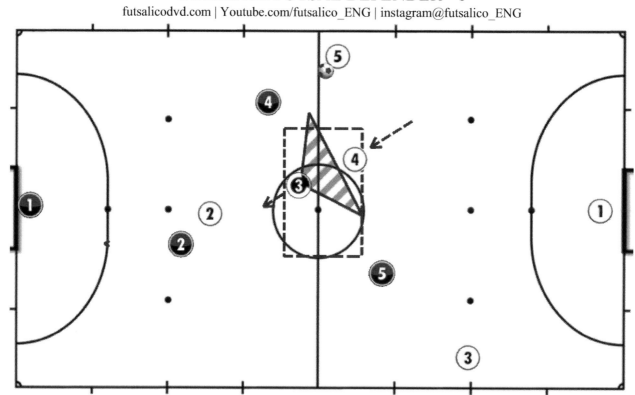

The scheme above shows us, that simple controlled retreat would be enough to "meet" white nr.4 and also - to cover the space in the middle (and not allow the pass through this zone).

I would also like to stress that the initial retreat in this situation would be a correct decision by a defender regardless of the defensive tactic (zonal, personal cover or any other). How far would black nr.3 go after that would differ from tactic to tactic, though. For example, here is how the further development of this situation would look like **in personal cover tactic**:

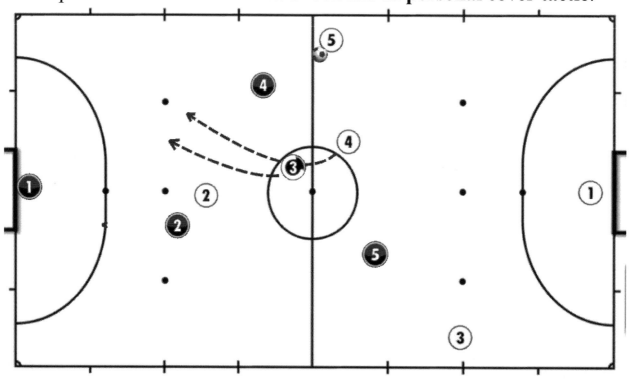

Here is, how defenders would be moving in a zonal system of defense:

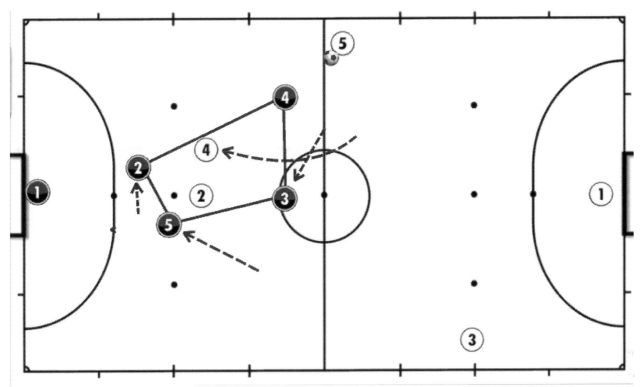

The scheme above shows black nr.3 going back towards the center and stays there to guard the middle zone. Black nr.2 moves slightly to the left to "meet" white nr.4. Black nr.5 moves to a position of the last defender. The most important in the case of zonal defense in this situation would be achieving control over all zones, position all defenders lower then the ball and create a diamond shaped formation towards the ball. All three objectives are met.

Now you can see, that the fact, that a defender was applying such principles as space orientation and peripheral vision, allowed black team to control the middle of the pitch and not allow white team to create a dangerous attack through the center. You have to remember, that regardless of the defensive tactic, you are using as a team, each and every defender's actions have to be focus on keeping the overall compactness of the team defense.

SPACE ORIENTATION TRAINING

How do you coach such thing as space orientation? Here are couple of drill, which will teach your players to keep their focus on the opponent with the ball and simultaneously - keep it compact at the back.

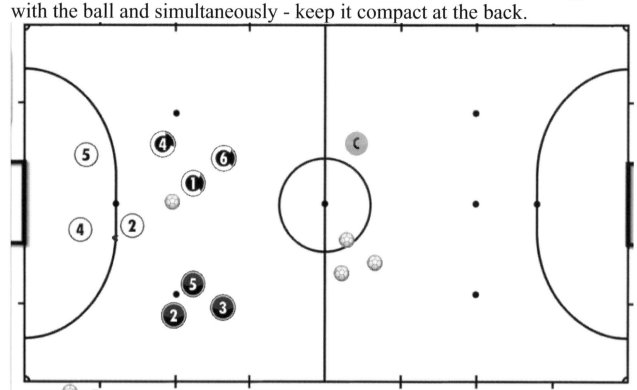

Objective: Teamplay in offense. Space orientation in defense.

Set-up: 3 teams of 3 field players each. No goal-keepers. No goals.

Equipment: 1/2 of the pitch. Vests (bibs) or 2-3 different colours (3 bibs of each colour). One ball. Keep all the rest of the balls near the pitch.

Intensity: High

Duration: 10 minutes x 3 times

Conditions: Random futsal game. Each player has maximum 3 touches on the ball. Two teams are always in possession of the ball and one team is always defending. Teams may switch roles during a game, but there always be 2 teams against 1.

How to play it: Two teams in possession have to make 15 consecutive passes. In the team lacks technical skills (first touch and passing are on low levels), then the objective fur such team may be 7 consecutive passes.

If there is an interception, then the team of a player, who lost the ball, becomes a defending team. The team of a player, who won the ball, becomes attacking team. No stops, dynamic play. So, if the ball gets intercepted and is still in play (did not leave the pitch), then players switch roles and keep playing.

What should a coach focus on? First of all, do not forget, what is is main objective of the drill. The main purpose is to teach players to defend against a certain opponent in a certain situation, while still making their contribution to team defense (by applying space orientation).

This drill makes defending players (who, by the way, are up against an opponent, who has numeric advantage of 6 players versus 3) support each other and also always think twice before throwing themselves on the opponent.

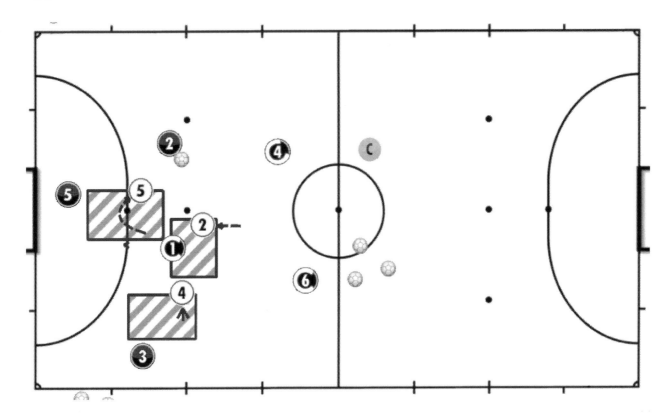

The scheme above shows you the same drill and illustrates the situation, which occurred during the play. White team applies space orientation. Take a bit of your time to analyze this situation.

If we take a more detailed look at this position, we would understand, that black nr.1 poses a big threat for a defense. If he receives a pass there, then both white nr.2 and white nr.5 are out of play immediately.

Therefore it is very important for white team to keep black nr.1 from receiving the ball in this position. Although how do you do it, when it's 3 up against 6? White nr.5 moves a bit forward towards the player with the ball and moved a bit from the side of black nr.5 (from the left). This immediately makes a pass to black nr.5 unlikely to happen.

White nr.2 made a couple of steps to his left and this helped him to narrow the corridor between himself and white nr.5. This way the pass to black nr.1 will also unlikely to happen.

White nr.4 made a small step forward, supporting his two partners just in case, if somehow the pass would still somehow reach black nr.1.

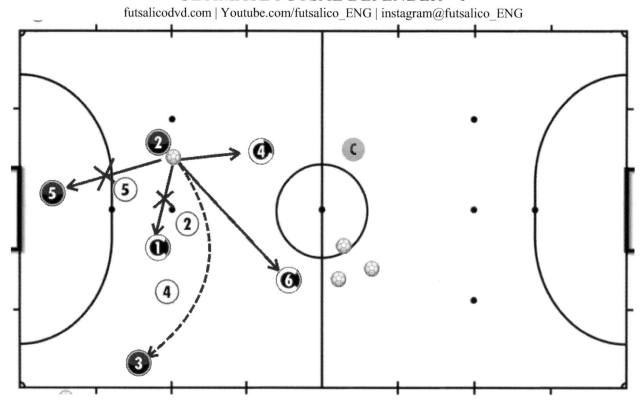

Scheme above shows you, that thanks to **correct** movements by defending team, their ability to apply the principle of peripheral vision, correct body positioning and last, but not the least - space orientation, defenders managed to block most of possible passing lines.

Black nr.1 and black nr.5 are unlikely to receive the ball (at least this would be very risky and hard to achieve for a white team). Black nr.2 can only receive the ball, which arrives high. Any high (lob) pass will be pretty easy to adjust to for a defense, because in this case the ball would be traveling slower. Therefore the passing line to black nr.3 is not that dangerous and defenders may let him loose a bit for now.

As a result, there are only two possible (safe) passes - to black nr.4 and to black nr.6. So that leaves us with 50% of possible passes being blocked. Note, that this was possible because of the correct positioning, body placing and space orientation by defenders. These movements, however, did not take much time or energy. At the same time the efficiency was enormous.

Let's now compare this situation with another (next scheme), where defenders are making incorrect movements and are not applying any space orientation. Players are basically playing intuitively.

So we can see, that white nr.5 is right in front of the player with the ball, completely ignoring any space orientation. White nr.4 is way too close to black nr.1, making his positioning absolutely useless. White nr.4 doesn't block any passing line and also won't be able to cover black nr.1 in case if he (or she) moves to any other position.

White nr.2 maybe thinks, that he took both attacking players simultaneously (meets black nr.4 and block the passing line to black nr.6). This is misleading, because the pass to black nr.4 can go absolutely easily. Regarding black nr.6, though...we can see, that defender didn't use any peripheral vision against him - black nr.2 can see the ball, but doesn't see the player.

Such small individual mistakes have a very big negative influence on the compactness of team defense. Fact is, that from this position a player with the ball can pass it to any of his teammates, except, may be, black nr.6. Although, black nr.6 can too move couple of steps to any side and easily receive the ball there. White nr.2 won't be able to see any movements of black nr.2 anyway.

4 passing directions from 5 possible. If we count the direction towards black nr.6 (who, as I just said, can easily move to any side and create passing line), then it would be 5 possible directions of 5!

So at least for sure we have 80% of possible passing lines open for a player with the ball to use. Such a defense can never be called compact and effective.

The drill, which I showed you previously is very useful not just in terms of training defense (both individual and team). It also allows to teach players to work against a opponent, who is both with and without the ball. This drill also teaches defenders take positions and on the pitch according to the principle of space orientation, while blocking any possible dangerous passing lines. All these factors help players take their efficiency to the next level.

Another benefit of this drill is it's **complexity**. Players are always in dynamics and therefore have to be keeping their focus on a very high level. Frequent change of roles (from defense to attack, from playing with the ball and without it, from attacking with superiority to defending with numeric disadvantage) and also change of direction of play, always keep players on the edge of their abilities and concentration. They learn to deal with different roles and situations and do it with cool head. This experience is very useful when it comes to playing a real match. This drill also makes players learn ot play efficiently in attack, although this would be a topic for different book (all my books can be found on futsalicodvd.com).

Another thing about balls. You have to use all the balls, which are at your disposal. One ball you need to play the drill, all other balls are your reserve. As soon as the main ball gets out of play, players should take the nearest ball and keep playing. It's necessary to keep the tempo of the game and overal intesity of the drill. Do not forget, that the job of any drill is to make it easier for players to play a real match situation.

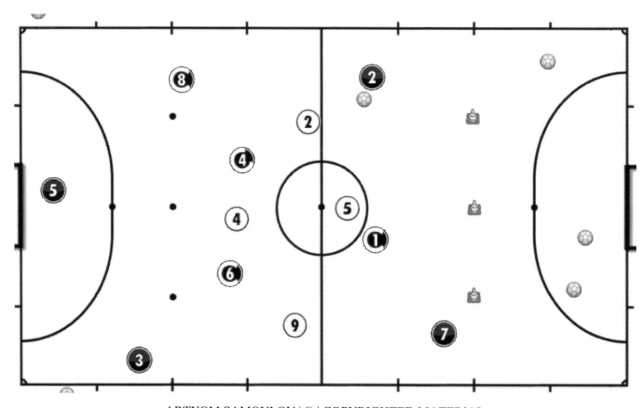

In you need to take this drill to another level, then use 75% of the pitch (scheme above) and the amount of players changes from three to four: 3 teams of 4 players. Other conditions remain the same.

Further on take this to the full pitch. This should be done it terms of one training session: 1/2 of the pitch, then 75% of the pitch and then - full pitch. Each stage 20 minutes (10 minutes x 2 times).

Another very important moment, which should be explained in this section is the role of the coach and his objectives. It is very important to stop players from time to time (it's better not to do it more often than once in 5 minutes, though). When players get frequently stopped, they tend to get anxious, cool down and lose the rhythm of the game.

Why do you need to stop players? It's necessary, so player's positioning could be corrected in real time. As a coach (captain, manager, playing coach etc.), you should remember, that any training session should have one single (main) objective. If this is learning or perfecting of individual (or collective) defensive actions, then each and every comment a coach makes should be about this topic.

How should you be stopping your player? Before the actual drill (during the explanation phase) tell your player, that in case if you make such a whistle (for example, single and very loud whistle) or clap in a certain way, all players should immediately stop at their positions!

The explanation and comments should be made, using the example (bad or good) of a certain player on the pitch. While you explain, make sure, all players listen carefully, because this is not a explanation for one certain player, but instead - for the whole team, using the example of one certain player. Encourage questions from players. This is the time and place for it!

Also very useful sometimes to let a certain player (choose anyone) to explain, what is done wrong and what is done right in this situation. When a player needs to explain it, he will have to choose correct words, concentrate on the topic and this will allow him to understand the situation even better. This is only useful, though, only in those cases, if the coach has already explained this kind of situation and now it repeated itself.

PLAYING AGAINST A BACK OF AN OPPONENT

If you want to learn to play against an opponent with a ball, you also have to be able to play against a player, who is turned with his back towards you. Opponent is shielding the ball from you with the help of his body, not allowing you to take the ball away from him. We will take a look a couple of situations, which will help you understand, how and what should a defender do in these types of situations:

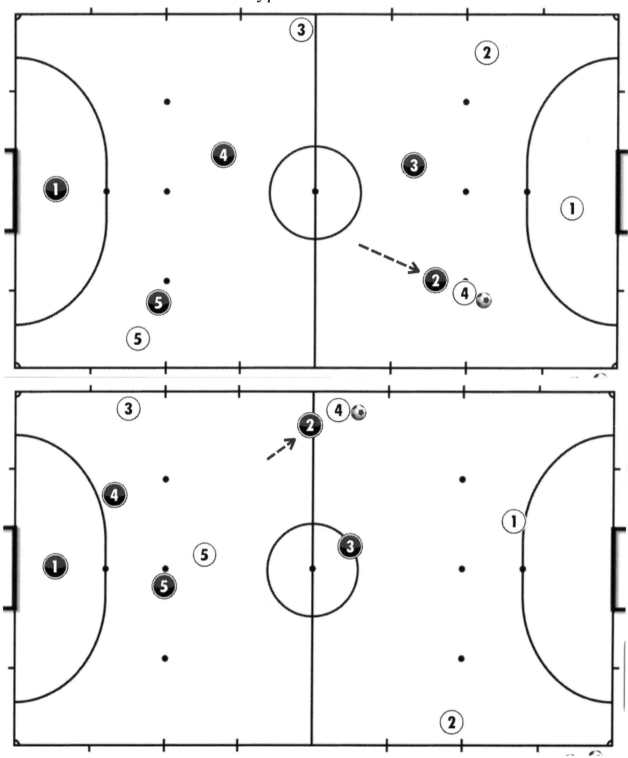

futsalicodvd.com | Youtube.com/futsalico_ENG | instagram@futsalico_ENG

On two schemes above you can see examples of situations, when a defending player is up against an opponent with a ball. What should a defender remember? The main risk for him is a potential turn of an opponent with a ball towards a defender. Situations, when an attacker has the ball at his feet and facing a defender, is the situation, where attacking player is in control of what's happening - not the defender. So therefore a defender has to avoid getting in these situations.

How can attacking player turn and what should be done to avoid this? There is a popular mistake, which defenders make in these situations: it's either positioning too far away from an attacker or getting way too close to him. These are main reasons, which usually lead to problems for defending team.

The best distance in this case would be 1.5-2 meters away from a player with the ball. If you are more than 2 meters away, attacker will be able to turn and face you. This will mean, that he now has an initiative. If this happen, for example, close to your goal (less than 12 meters away from the goal), this would be a potentially dangerous situation for a defensive team. A player with a decent shooting skill is able to score from such **distance**.

If you are, on the other hand, too close (closer than 1.5m) to a player with the ball, he will be able to use your body as a leaning point, make a faint move to one side and then turn to another.

I would like to illustrate this with an example of defense against a pivot. For the most of the time pivot is playing with his back towards opponents goal. He usually in the most dangerous position - right in front of the goal. He is the most **skillful** player in terms of the skill of shielding the ball with the body.

Here's how you **should not be** playing against a pivot:

In this position defender is **exposed to a turn of a pivot.** Defender can simply be used as a leaning point for a turn.

Here is what can happen, if a pivot **turns** into a shooting position:

Now let us see, how a defender should be playing against a pivot. This is an example of an effective defense and correct body position:

How can you evaluate, what is too close, what is too far and what is a correct position? The indicator of an optimal distance may the your hand, which is put forward and touches a pivot.

You can put your hand forward and touch the back of an opponent. This will let him know, you are right here, watching him. Also this will allow you to be in approximately 1.5m distance from him. Like that:

You may think, that using your hands like that is against the rules and is a fault. It's not. I would say there is a thin line between the fault and playing by the rules. You have to know the difference. Professional players know it and use it all the time. If you do not push a player with your hands, if do not grab him or hit him, that means you are playing according to the rules.

HOW TO COVER YOUR RESPECTIVE PLAYERS

It's not that easy to detect, how close or how far away you should be from your respective player. I would like to suggest you to use two criteria to make it easier. Based on these two aspects (criteria) you can **evaluate, whether you are in a correct position:**

1. **Whether a player has a ball (or not)**
2. **How far an opponent with a ball is from your goal**

Here is example (the ball is on opponent's half - far away from our goal):

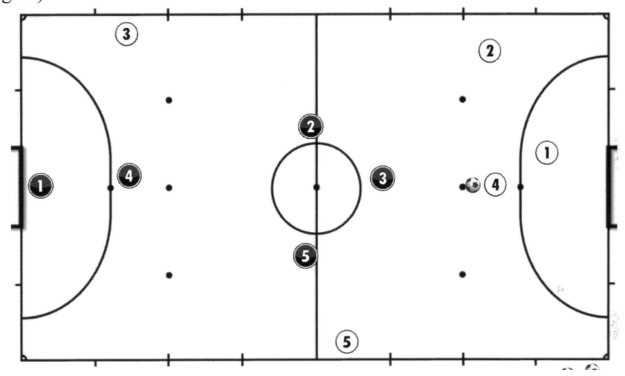

In this situation (scheme above) black team is using a personal cover in formation 1-1-2-1 (defensive zone is 75% or 3/4 of the pitch). Black nr.4, who is responsible for the covering of an attacking pivot (white nr.3), at this very moment is pretty much away from white nr.3. Defender is in a correct position, because at this very moment his respective player (white nr.3) is not posing the biggest danger for a defense. First of all white nr.3 doesn't have the ball and second - he is more away from the ball than any other of opponent's players.

At this very moment the potential danger coming from a white nr.3 is the same as from white nr.5, for example. White nr.5 potentially can outrun black nr.5 down the left flank. This can lead to a situation, where black nr.4 (last defender) would have to move to the right flank to meet white nr.5.

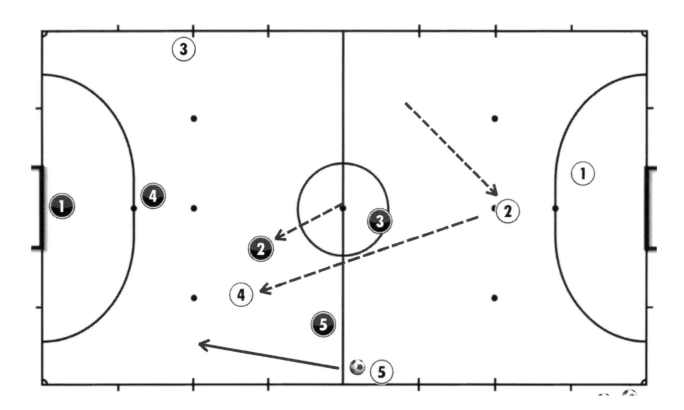

If we take a look at the scheme above, we can see the potential attack down the left flank. White nr.5 already has a ball. White nr.4 makes a run down the left flank in order to try and receive the pass there (this kind of an attacking combination has a name, buy the way and is called "parallel").

If this happens, what should black nr.4 do then? First of all he has to take a look, where black nr.2 (his teammate) is moving. We can see, that black nr.2 has let his respective player loose a bit, but overall still has a control over the situation. In this case the pass to white nr.3 is unlikely to happen, but still - possible. Therefore black nr.4 should not be moving towards the right flank (at least at this very moment), but instead should stay where he is.

If white nr.3 moves to the center, then black nr.4 would meet him there. If the pass goes to white nr.3 (to the left flank), then our last defender will just make a couple of steps towards his respective opponent and will be in possession to contain him. Like that:

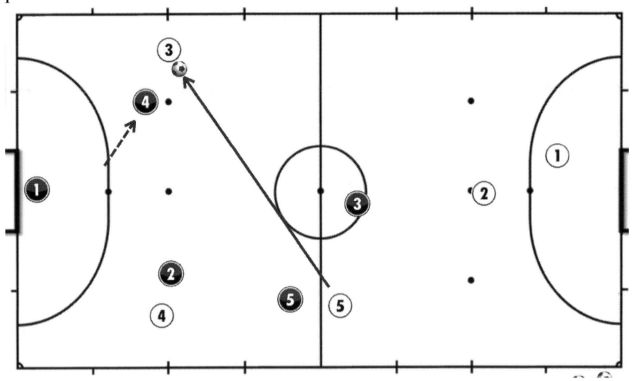

There can also be a situation, when a defender can give his respective opponent some freedom. That is a case, when, for example, black nr.3 was able to turn the the player with the ball to the **flank**:

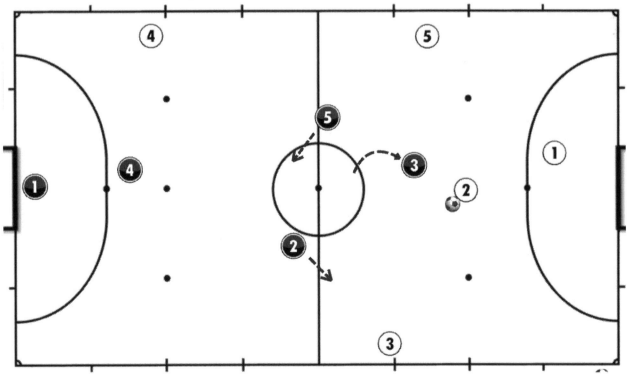

Scheme above shows us, that black player nr.3 moves slightly from the left and white nr.2 has to turn to his left. This is a moment for black nr.2 and nr.5 to correct their positions. Black nr.5 for example can move a bit away from white nr.5, because the pass to the right attacking flank is unlikely to happen. This slight adjustment by black nr.5 will also allow him to cover the middle of the pitch and therefore - make overall team defensive system much more compact.

Black nr.2, on the other hand, has to move a bit closer to white nr.3. This is necessary, because the possibility of a pass to the left attacking flank now becomes higher. It is important, though, not to come too close, so white nr.3 doesn't go behind defender's back (next scheme):

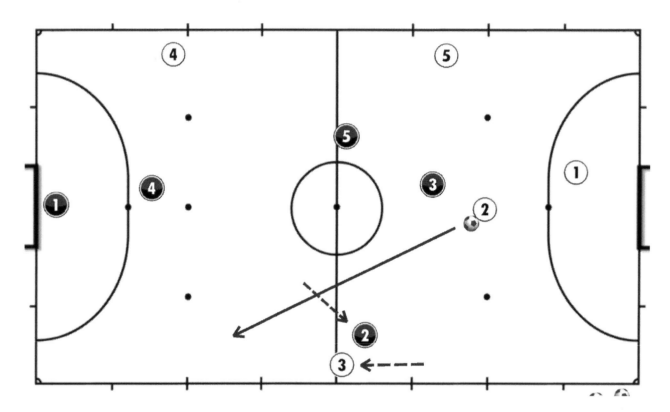

futsalicodvd.com | Youtube.com/futsalico_ENG | instagram@futsalico_ENG

HOW TO PLAY IN A PARALLEL MOVEMENT

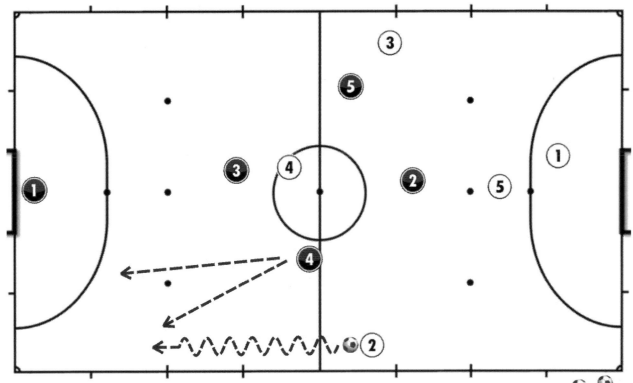

Scheme above shows us a situation, when player in possession of the ball decides to dribble down the left flank with and objective to make a shot a goal. Black nr.4 has different options. At this point, though, it's not wise to get closer to white nr.2. It would be better to take the parallel course, keeping safe distance of 2-3m. This will not allow a player with the ball to create a comfortable corridor (opportunity) for a shot. Second - this positioning by black nr.4 will keep the defensive construction and overall defensive system's compactness. This will also let a defender to avoid the risk of being outplayed.

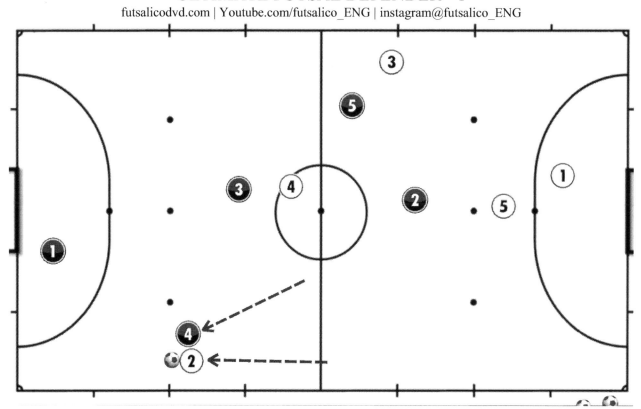

Scheme above shows us an example of **incorrect final position** of black nr.4. Defender ended up in this position because of his wrong vector of movement. he wasn't going in parallel, but instead - was moving straight towards white nr.2. Let's see, why this is a risky play by the defender:

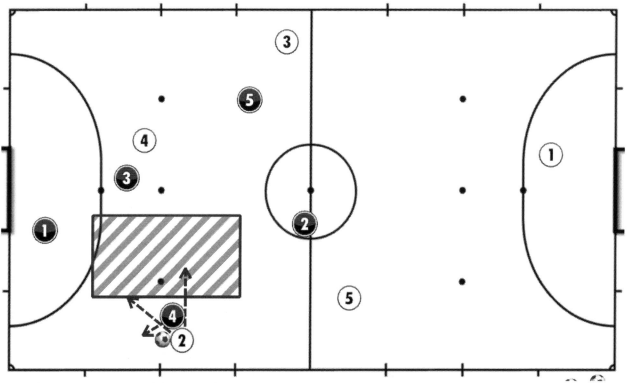

White nr.2 in this position can easily push the ball towards the goal, crossing trajectories and leaving black nr.4 behind him. This is a situation, where a defender can just be in a way of an attacking player (without even tackling him) and this could cause a collision and fault. Such a fault and in this position would almost certainly mean a yellow card or (which is may be even worse) - white nr.2 going one on one with a goalie.

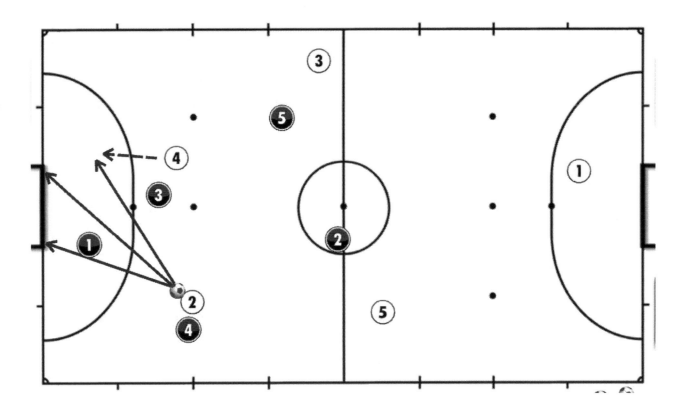

If white nr.2 stops and moves towards the center (scheme above), there is a big variety of possibilities for him. Each of these possibilities would immediately mean big problems for a defending side. Besides the potential fault (followed by a yellow or even red card) and a dangerous set-piece, white nr.2 could be in a position, where it would be easier to score, then not to score.

Another extreme scenario would be, if a defender is not moving towards white nr.2, but instead - is being too passive and staying too far away. You can not be simply moving in parallel while keeping to big distance from a player with a ball. The ideal position of a defender here would be the one, where he controls an attacker, avoid risks of being outplayed, but is still "always around". Defender should be letting a player with the ball know, that if he makes any mistake, defender will immediately be there to take the ball away from him.

If a defender is too far, then this could lead to an easy shot at goal (next two schemes):

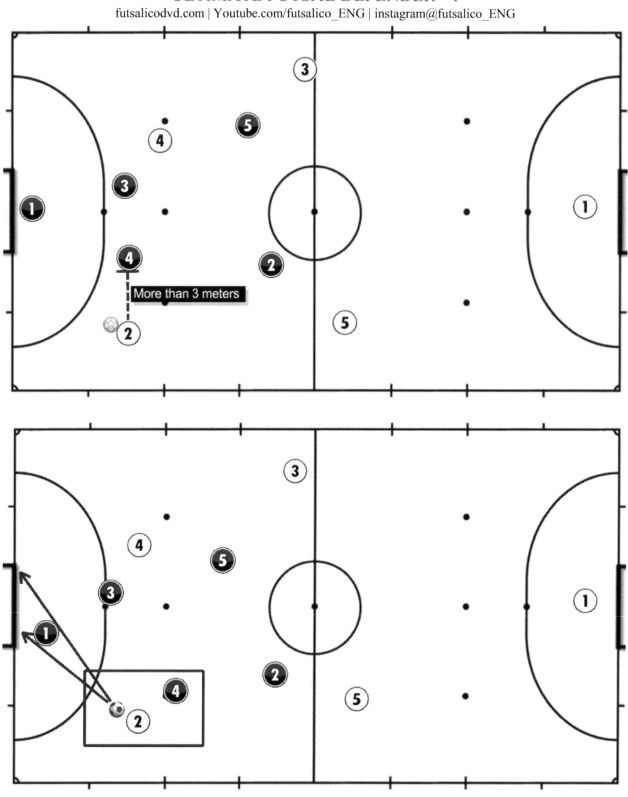

Here is how a defender **should be playing** in this case:
- keep the **distance** of 2-3 meters to a player with the ball
- keep the same tempo as a player with the ball (that would also mean - to accelerate, when attacker accelerates and lower the tempo, when attacker slows it down)

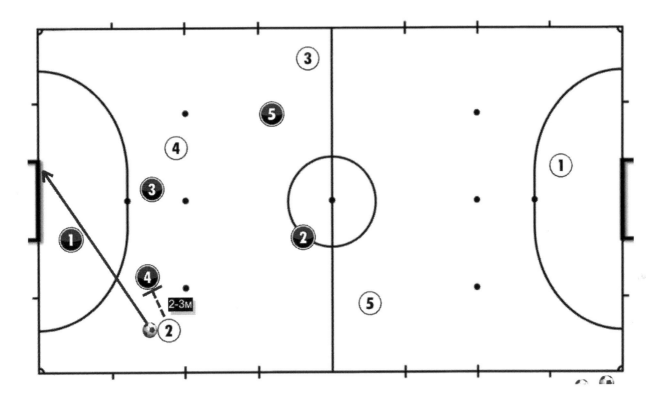

Goalkeeper should be covering the closest post, but a defender should be positioning himself near the potential line of the shot. Not directly on the line, though, but very close to it. Just enough to be able **to reach the ball with his foot** in case and an attacker makes a shot.

futsalicodvd.com | Youtube.com/futsalico_ENG | instagram@futsalico_ENG

TACKLING: HOW, WHEN AND WHY

Loads of mistakes are made by defenders exactly, when they tackle their opponent. There are certain factors, which the decision to tackle (or not) should be depending on. So you could understand these factors better, let's divide them into 3 groups:

- **Group nr.1: Factors, which are related to a tackling player (defender)**
- **Group nr.2: Factors, related to a player, who gets tackled (attacker)**
- **Group nr.3: External factors**

I would like to say right away, that I won't be wasting time here on explaining group nr.2 factors in this section. I will do that in the section called "How to defend against a skillful opponent". Instead I will concentrate on group nr.1 and group nr.3.

- **Group nr.1: Factors, which are related to a tackling player (defender)**

Fitness and endurance

The decision, whether to tackle an opponent with the ball, should not be spontaneous. I'd say, that only professional and experienced futsalers can sometimes make intuitive and spontaneous decisions on the pitch. That is because their habits, skill and huge number of games behind them, allows them to do it. Professionals, by the way, are those players, who make their living out of playing futsal - receive money for it.

The most interesting thing about is, that professionals are usually the one, who make their decisions on the field, based on their knowledge of main futsal concepts. They also have enough discipline to follow tactical objectives of the coach. Most of their actions are calculated and rational.

An average amateur player usually doesn't have much experience, lacks futsal tactical knowledge (which doesn't allow him to read the game well and quickly) and his level of discipline is not enough to make calculated and rational decisions on the pitch. Most of decisions, amateur player makes, are very much influenced by the tiredness, stress and emotions.

Amateur player would often have trouble timing his tackles, which would result in unnecessary fouls, lost positions, problems for other teammates, who have to cover for him etc. In this section of the book I will give you some indicators, which will allow you to evaluate the situation better and make rational defensive decisions. Think of it as a road map, which guides you through different situations in the game.

Based on my experience, amateur players often have problems, whet it comes to tackling. How do you tackle? When do you tackle? Tackle or wait for an opponent to make a mistake: what's better and in what situation? I will try to give you an answer to these questions.

Try to **tackle less** (and instead prefer good positioning, zone covering, containing, waiting for opponent's mistake etc.) **if you:**
- **are physically unfit**
- **have low endurance**
- **are slow**
- **cannot read the game well (or do it too slow)**
- **don't know how to the tackling technically**
- **don't know, how to time your tackle**

Tackling is not just a technical element of futsal (skill), which a futsal player learns and then perfects during his whole futsal career. It's not enough to know, how to do it!

Tackling involves a physical contact with an opponent. As a defender you have to be able to actually go shoulder to shoulder with your opponent. You have to be capable of shielding the ball, using your body to fight for the space. You have to be able to stay on your feet, when opponent pushes you. It's necessary to time your tackle and be fast enough to do it etc.

You also have to understand, that after the tackle (the fight for the ball), regardless of the outcome (lost or won the ball), you have to be able to continue playing (defending or attacking). Therefore if you spent all your energy in the fight for the ball and cannot continue playing effectively enough, then probably you should have never got into this tackle. Even if you won the ball in it.

Every factor, I mentioned, has to be taken into consideration, when it comes to planning your preparation for a game or for a season. Each training process should involve drills, which help players work towards mentioned objectives.

Physical preparation is very underestimated. Many amateur teams do not have training processes and coaches. Most of such teams start their training sessions by dividing into two groups of 5 players and just play against each other. Sometimes there is some kind of warm-up, but it's not a proper one. Players are just passing or individually dribble the ball and shoot. This may continue for 10 minutes and then they play futsal for the rest of the time.

This is not enough. This kind of approach won't allow you to progress, won't bring you any closer to achieving your goals in futsal (individual or team). What I am suggesting is to include physical preparation in your training time. High fitness level of players may someday play a big part in success. Fit team is more stable, it can resist opponent of any level, because fitness sometimes overcome skill.

Over 8 years ago I was training one of amateur teams in Latvia. I encountered a situation, when most players didn't have a high level of skill. These were normal regular guys, who just liked to play futsal and had two "training sessions" per a week. These guys were playing like that for couple of years. They never had a proper training process. Training sessions just included a lot of playing futsal (no warm-up, no objectives, no drills, no preparation, no tactics, no goals - just fun).

Don't get me wrong, I have nothing against having fun. It's just, if you are in futsal for a company of friends, spending time together, have some movement from time to time, it's all good. It's your own choice and I am not the one to school you about your decisions. On the other hand, what always amazed me it's, how such guys get angry, sad and sometimes completely down, when they join a tournament and start losing big.

To me it's always been like this: you either forget about a training process and enjoy your time or crate a proper approach, training process, objectives, plan your training sessions etc.

If you chose the first option (no preparation), it may be just playing with your friends once or twice a week or even going into a tournament. But then, if you are losing a game in a tournament, don't be sad. If a team, which doesn't have a training process, objectives, squad selection, drills, analysis etc, loses a game in a tournament it's not a surprise. At least to me it isn't. Just forget the result and move on. You are not in here for result.

But in cases, if you feel sad, angry or unsatisfied with a result, then may be (if you are a player of such team) you have to find a new team. Team, which has a coach, which has a training process and has goals to achieve. You can also create a training process in your team too. It's not that hard. All you need is a will to do it and some knowledge.

So I get a team at my disposal and first thing I do is implement a training process. Now we have a proper warm-up, we have preparation drills, main drills, we play a game at the end of the session for only 10-20 minutes.

Sometimes we even have objectives for this game too - it's not just playing. We also have a warm-down and physical preparation. We gather additional time once a week outside to run, sprint and have core exercises. We now are checking our weight weekly to stay fit. The most important, though - we have a goal now!

I didn't start talking about this team just for nothing. This is an example, I would like share with you. This was the team, which managed to overturn bad statistics (and start getting results) and one of the main reason for that was it's good physical preparation!

This wasn't a revolution, which I made there. I just implemented a discipline, goal-oriented approach, focus and gave a basic physical preparation to players. All the rest was up to the players. It's was their job now to go out there and give it all on the pitch. I give players all the credit for their effort and thank them for trusting me.

In couple of weeks we started to get points. We managed to overcome the decline and started to become more stable. We started losing less goals and with that came confidence! Those, games, which would usually finish 3-3 or 5-5, we would be winning now. In those games, where we would be equal with our opponent skills and experience wise, we would be able to win now.

I remember a game, which for 36 minutes held a result 0-0! Those, who play amateur futsal, know how unusual this is in this sport. Especially on amateur level, where defensive organization is usually not at their best. Thanks to our fitness levels and discipline, we were able to stay more focused then our opponent and scored from two set-plays at the very end of the game. This match finished 2-0 and we got very valuable 3 points. Some might say, that scoring from a set-play is lucky. I assure you, it's not the luck. To score on a set-piece (especially at the end of the game) you have to be focused, time all your movements and passes right. We played our prepared combination, which would involve simultaneous coordinated movements of all four field players.

We were able to draw against stronger teams and even managed to get two victories in 3 matches with two best teams of the tournament (one became a champion, another took a second place). From the lower end of the table we got into top 4 in just 6 games.

Now we had something else, which is even better, then beating stronger teams. We had a belief now, we had confidence. It came from our discipline on the pitch, high fitness levels of our players and good results on the pitch.

We had a certain approach to the game: "Give it all. Stay cool and work hard. For every ball. Every minute of the match. No matter the result." I tried to explain my players, that if we spend our time here (preparing on training session, getting to the match, playing and getting back home), then we have to give it all. Even if we lose, we are going to have no regrets. Because we gave it all. Our consciousness is clear.

What else does physical fitness give you? It allows players to go up against skillful teams and really hope for a result. We became a very difficult team to beat. Defensively strong, disciplined, with high levels work-rate. Even after losing a position or being outplayed, our opponent's players knew, we are immediately "on their tale". When an opponent with the ball sees, that a player, who he just got passed, is back to fighting for the ball and already behind his back, opponent knows he has not space for mistakes and has to hurry up. This makes him get nervous, makes him doubt himself, leads him to making mistakes.

I wouldn't say, I managed to get a team to the next level on a long-term. We achieve the maximum at the time and place. Team needed a reconstruction. This was a team, which had an owner and I was a coach in it. Owner and me, we had different long-term objectives and ways to achieve them. Therefore I quit a team. This by the way for the first experience for me on a position of a coach in an amateur team, which didn't belong to me (I was not the owner and founder of it). Although I managed teams with owners again, most of my next teams I was creating on my own. I needed a full control to be able to implement all my ideas.

There were teams, which I trained for a specific goal (like projects). For example, I coached a bank team once with an objective to get to Corporate tournament and try to win it. I coached some teams, which had objectives, for example, to get to a higher division etc. Regardless of the type of the team or objective, my main condition was always - to have a "Card Blanche" (full control) over the training process and the squad.

Back to the team I was talking, though. The focus on physical fitness and discipline helped us big in that season. We managed to stop the decline, stop losing points. I took a team in the middle of the season. From the beginning of that season until I became a coach, 14 games were played, 10 points won, 24 scored, 60 goals conceded! In that season I was in charge of the team for 12 more games. In those we managed to get 24 points, score 51 goal and lose only 26.

For the first 14 games of the season the statistics of the team (where was no training process, no competition for a place in the squad etc.) looked like this:

- **goal difference: minus 36**
- **an average of 4.23 goals conceded per a game**
- **an average of 1.71 goals scored per a game**
- **an average of 0.71 points earned per a game**

When the competition for a place in a squad was implemented, one of the main criteria was the physical condition of players. This played a decisive role in the change of statistics, which in the next 12 games looked like this:

- **goal difference: plus 25**
- **an average of 2.17 goals conceded per a game**
- **an average of 4.25 goals scored per a game**
- **an average of 2 points earned per a game**

I am giving you this stats now to brag or anything. I want you to understand, how physical preparation, discipline and a clear goal might chance things. We changed our approach to the game: the focus was now on compact defense on 1/2 of the pitch and quick counter-attacking play.

Players learned the basics of defensive play and counter-attacks. This tactics was ideal for a team, consisted of players, who were physically fit, disciplined and eager to prove themselves, they can win things. We were tight at the back and took advantage of opponent's mistakes.

Now let us move on to another aspect, which is highly important for a defender: **technical-tactical factors:**

1. **Defensive support** (when a defense is set in a way, that every player can always count on his team-mate's help in case, if gets outplayed or loses positioning) - we are going to talk about it in details in the section "How to play against a quick and skillful opponent"
2. Ability of defending players to **adjust their positioning** according to where other teammates are.
3. **Distance to an opponen**t
4. **Tackling**

I think now is the best time to explain you the term laterality.. This is a term, every futsaler should be familiar with. In full detail I am talking about this term in series of book on futsal attacking tactics and concepts. This term, though is also important, when it comes to defending.

The term laterality refers to the preference most humans show for one side of their body over the other. Examples include left handedness / right handedness, left footedness / right footedness. In futsal this would mean, that every player has a preferred (strongest) foot and also - preferred (strongest) side of the body.

The main job of any futsal player is to try to avoid the influence of laterality on his game. Consider laterality as a weakness, which doesn't allow you to perform at your full potential. One of the most important jobs of any player is to improve his weak foot or weak side of the body as much as it is possible.

Attacking player should be able to play with both his feet with the same amount of confidence and effectiveness. At least he (or she) has to work towards it. Even if your weakest foot is not as effective and strong as your strongest foot, you at least have to take your weakest foot to certain level, where you would be able to use it without any thinking and implement all your ideas on the pitch, regardless of what foot your are playing with.

Laterality in defense would mean that some players are using one side of their body better than the other. Defenders should not take their position against an opponent based on what the preferred side of their body is. They have to take positions regardless of that. If you need to turn your body to the left, because the situation tell you to do it, you should do it without any hesitation. Often defenders take incorrect positions, make incorrect turns and lose precious time because they have a preferred side. We will take a look at some examples, which will illustrate the things I am talking about.

Here is a picture (above), where a blue player (if you are reading this book in a black and white colours - a darker player on the side line) has just played a pass to his partner (nr.14). After the pass, he starts his run towards the opponent's goal down the right attacking flank.

A defender (he is circled on the picture) **has a clear laterality** (his right side is stronger, than his left side), which doesn't allow him to make a correct turn. He tries to gain control of the situation by turning to his opponent with his strongest side. As a result of this he will lose time, balance and the fight for the space.

Here is another situation (picture above). Nr.14 makes a pass forward. The defender (circled) is already in a bad position, because he has to be at least facing the ball. This is not the worst thing though. What is important is to take a look at how he is going to turn. Let's take a look at how situation develops:

Previous picture shows us, that a defender can see the pass going towards the side line. If this player didn't have laterality, he would be able to use both side of his body with the same amount of efficiency. He would also be able to turn towards the ball by turning to his left. This would allow him to turn faster. This would also allow him to intercept the ball with his left foot. If he would do that he would be in total control of the situation: he would see the ball, most probably would be able to intercept it and start a counter-attack.

The picture above shows us, that a defender decided to turn towards the ball with his strongest (right) side and this resulted into losing load of time and space. The effectiveness of such play is very **low**. It's not, what the game situation asks from the player. It's the case, where a player doesn't, what is more suitable for himself.

When a defender tackles, it's important for him to not cross his feet. He always has to play with the closest foot to the ball. There are some cases, though, when this rules doesn't work too, but most of the time it does.

The job of any coach is to get his players to the state, when when their laterality doesn't influence the decision-making on the pitch. At the end of this section I would like to give you a drill to achieve that.

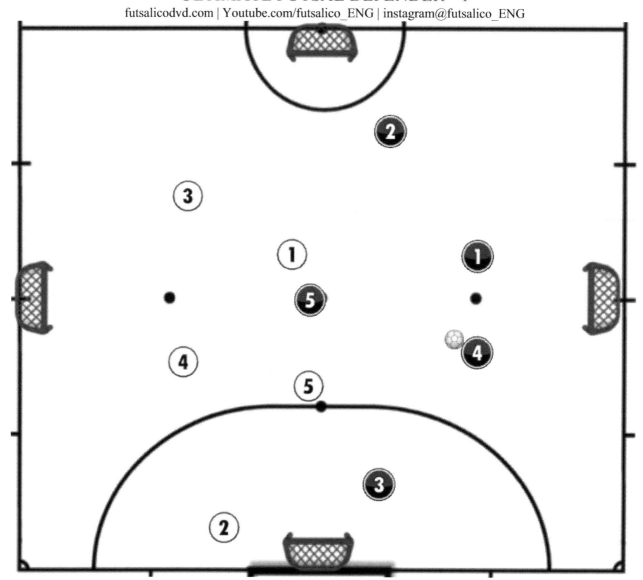

Set-up:
2 teams of 5-6 field players. No goal-keepers. 1/2 of the pitch.

Equipment: One ball. 4 goals.

Intensity: High

Duration: 10 minutes x 3 times

Conditions:
Each team defends two goals. You can tell each team, which is their two goals randomly, but it would be better if goals are close to one another. To make the drill more diverse, players can be told to use maximum three touches on the ball.

futsalicodvd.com | Youtube.com/futsalico_ENG | instagram@futsalico_ENG

This drill would allow to change tempo and roles of players frequently. Just as this happens during the match. This is exactly, what we want. Players would have to turn very often to adjust their positioning according to what happens on the pitch.

What does a coach have to remember, when it comes to this drill? He (or she) has to tell players, what the objective of the drill is. What players would be learning to do. Coach has to show players, how it should and should not be done.

During the drill itself, coach has to stop players from time to time (not too often though, so the drill doesn't lose it's dynamics) to correct their positioning and illustrate a problem (using the example of a certain player, who just made a mistake by turning incorrectly). When players see the real example, for them it's easier to understand, what was done wrong.

Group nr.2: Factors, related to a player, who gets tackled (attacker)

When a defender faces an opponent with the ball, he has to remember the laterality concept. Laterality is also the can, when it comes to dribbling the ball. Defender has to evaluate the situation and try to catch the moment, when his opponent's decision is **influenced by his laterality.**

Let's take a look, at how an attacking player should (and should not) be using his feet. This will help you to know, when to tackle such a player. So, if I would have to put it in two words, I would say, that ideally a player with the ball should move the ball to his left with the left foot and to his right - with the right foot.

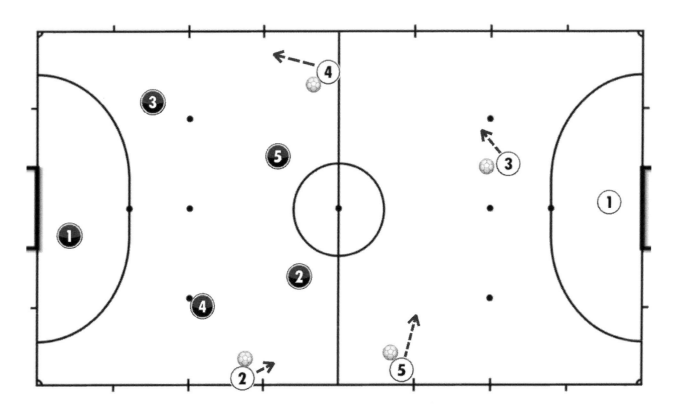

Scheme above shows us some examples of movements of the player with the ball, where he has to move the ball to his right with his right foot. Positions, which you see here are irrelevant (in other positions the same principles would be applied). If you move the ball to your right with your left foot, it's not restricted too. Although the efficiency of such play would be lower.

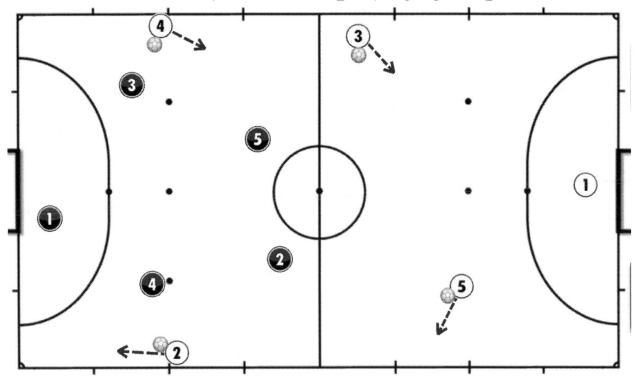

Same logic is applied to the left foot: if you move to the left (scheme above), you should be using your left foot. Important note, though. What I talk about here are situations, when a player with the ball is facing an opposite goal. That means, for example, that a pivot, who receives the ball while facing his own goal (turned with his back to opponent's goal), may ignore laterality principle.

Why we would need to use a certain foot while going to a certain side, anyway? As I say already, it's because we would be more efficient like that. Would not lose precious time and balance. Attacking player, who is using a correct foot, will always be in a more stable position and that means - ready to react to a changing situation on the pitch.

Why would the topic of laterality in attack be important in this book, though? The thing is that at the moment, when a defender sees, that his opponent (with the ball) is using incorrect foot, this would be the moment to tackle.

I am not saying, you should throw yourself in a tackle at the very moment, when you see your opponent is using incorrect foot. Consider opponent's mistake as a trigger (signal, indicator) for you, that this might be favorable situation to try and get the ball away from your opponent.

So if as a defender, you see this happening and at the moment, you yourself are in a good position, within a good perfect distance and ready to tackle, then this would be a moment to do that.

Here is an example of attacking player moving the ball to his left, while using his right foot:

On the picture above you can see a situation which is favorable for a defender to make a tackle.

Picture above shows you another situation, when an attacking player uses wrong foot to dribble the ball to his side. He dribble to his left with his right foot. You can see, that attacking player crosses his feet, while dribbling the ball to his side - this is a **trigger** (invitation) for a defender to tackle. If at this point a defender feels ready to do it, he should **tackle**.

Picture above shows you an example of using a **correct** foot. Player uses his left foot to go to the left. This is a good practice, because the player doesn't lose any time and is maximum **efficient**.

Picture above shows us another good example of a **good play** by an attacking player. Player moves the ball to the left, while using his left foot.

So I guess, you got the idea. I must say though, that such triggers (signal) are usually clear for those players, who have a big experience in futsal. Mostly these are professional futsalers. On amateur (and youth) level such things often go unnoticed. Therefore, when kids are still young a coach should already help them become less reliable on their laterality. In case, if you coach amateurs grown-ups, then when it comes to improving their skills, one of the first things to do is to help them develop their weak side of the body. Both in terms of offense and defense. Players should improve their body positioning, using correct foot, make correct turns, improve their peripheral vision etc.

A coach has to teach players to take offensive position and show attacking intention, when they have the ball at their feet. Players also have to know, what is a correct defensive body position and should be able to shows their defensive intentions, when they are up against an attacking opponent.

Here is an example of **bad defensive intention**:

Here is an example of a **good defensive intention:**

Group nr.3: External factors

When I say "external factors", I mean conceptual playing philosophy of a coach, game plan for a certain game and the game situation. These factors influence the dicision-making process of a futsal player.

For example, coach has a preferred way of playing and coaches his teams accordingly. For example, if the philosophy of a coach a compact defense, discipline all over the pitch, no unnecessary risks etc, then this approach would be translated to players on the pitch. This will eventually influence a decision of a player whether to intercept the ball, tackle an opponent or contain, wait, control and take more conservative approach.

On the other hand, there are coaches, who would encourage players to press high, go into tackles and try to attack the lines of the pass and intercept the ball with a bigger aggression. That is up the coach to decide, how his team player. That is normal. The coach (captain, manager, playing-coach) will be only judged by the result.

If it comes to me, for example, I would always analyze my opponents before the game. In cases, when I see, that players mostly do not have high level of futsal skills and tend to lose the ball in after 3-4 passes, I would instruct my team not to take unnecessary risks. It's not need, because opponents will most probably eventually lose the ball anyway.

In this case my job would to instruct my team to control passing lines, stay compact and focus on space orientation, provide support for partners and avoid unnecessary risks.

When I see a necessity to play with bigger **aggression** (for example in those cases, when my opponent's are skillful players and like to prepare their attack), I would instruct my team accordingly. In this case we would be using any opportunity to engage in the fight for the ball, attack passing lines and take a more intense and aggressive approach to the game. This also can happen, when my team is losing and there is not much time to score. I would tell my guys to try to go into risky challenges on the opponent's half of the pitch, but avoid doing that on our half.

If opponent likes long combinations and arrives to my half of the pitch after 7-8 passes are already made, there is a high possibility, that there already be some open spaces in my defensive system. that would also mean, that we are playing right into it (the play goes according to opponent's plan). This is not what I want. So it's better if my team risks on opponent's half (while still being pretty compact) and doesn't allow my opponent to even start their combination, than deals with them on my half

futsalicodvd.com | Youtube.com/futsalico_ENG | instagram@futsalico_ENG

of the pitch. In the end it is up to you to decide, how you play. There is no one correct way of doing it. That's why futsal is so interesting.

There is a factor of a certain game situation too. Let's say, the plan for a match is to not risk a lot, stay compact and "meet" our an opponent at the centered of the pitch (middle line). At the same time, there might be a situation during the game, when good opportunity to press and play aggressively arrives unexpectedly. For example, opponent's player made a bad first touch or his partners haven't provided good support for him. If a defender is nearby and ready to tackle, then he should. Regardless of the team's overall approach for the match.

There is also a factor of a score. If, for instance, there is no way your team can allow to concede a goal (last minutes of the game, you are winning and you badly need three points), then it would also influence the dicision-making process of players. It should, at least. Players should be more careful and take almost no risk at all.

TACTICAL TRAPS

This section of the book is going to concentrate on, how your opponent's players can be moved to certain directions. Even, when a defending team doesn't have the ball, it still has an opportunity to control, how the play goes. It can be achieved with the help of such small thing as the position of defender's feet and body.

There are several reasons, why you would try and encourage your opponents to develop their attack to certain directions. This type of "encouragement" is called a tactical trap. **Tactical traps are set with different objectives.** There are **4 main ones:**

1. **Turning opponent's attack to the direction of the strongest side of a defender**
2. **Turning opponent's attack to the direction of his (opponent's) weakest side**
3. **Turning opponent's attack towards the flank**
4. **Turning opponent's attack towards the center**

TACTICAL TRAP NR.1

Turning opponent's attack to the direction of the strongest side of a defender

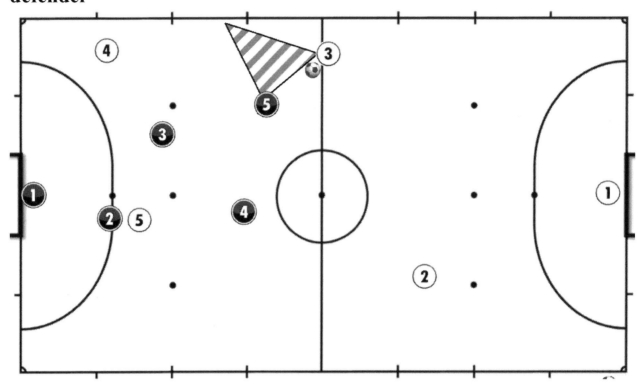

Previously in this book we already talked about moving our opponent towards the strongest side of a defender. In short, the main idea is that defender can choose, what is his preferred side (right or left) and then prevent opponent from going to another (not prefered) side.

If for example, a black nr.5 (scheme above) wants to defend in the area to his left, then he should encourage white nr.3 to to that way. What is the way to do that? Simply approach your opponent slightly from the right side, cut this path. Most probably the player with the ball will choose to avoid a collision (possible tackle, which may lead to loosing the ball) and as a result - will move to your left.

Just a slight change of the position of your body and feet (defender's right foot would be put a bit forward and left leg would stay a bit behind) can let the defender achieve the objective.

To take a look at the example of such play analysis, please turn to certain section of the book in the chapter "Opponent with the ball - Positioning on the pitch".

TACTICAL TRAP NR.2

Turning opponent's attack to the direction of his (opponent's) weakest side

First of all, let's deal with the "why" part. Why do you need this tactical trap and what it's for? Every opponent has strongest and weakest side of his body, strongest foot and strongest hand. For right-footed players it's easier to play with their right foot. Left-footed players play better with their left foot. It's just a habit, which each of us develops from the childhood.

The job of a defender is to detect, which foot of his (or her) opponent is the strongest and make him (or her) play with the weakest foot or move his (or her) weakest side.

For a right-footed player:
- strongest side is right side
- preferred direction is right
- preferred foot is right

For a left-footed player:
- strongest side is left side
- preferred direction is left
- preferred foot is left

Now let us focus on the "**how**" part. How should a defender play against a certain type of players? Let's take a look at some examples.

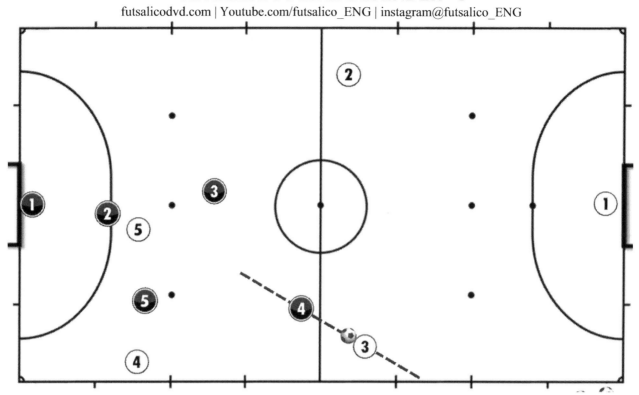

Black nr.4 "meets" white nr.3. Let us imagine a line between the ball and the center of the goal. At this point (scheme above) a defender is located strictly on this line. Let's call it a starting (default) position.

Let us imagine, that our opponent with the ball is a "righty". So the job of the defender is to make him move to the his (or her) left - to the uncomfortable side and foot. How does a defender do that? He should approach a defender slightly from opponent's right side (next scheme):

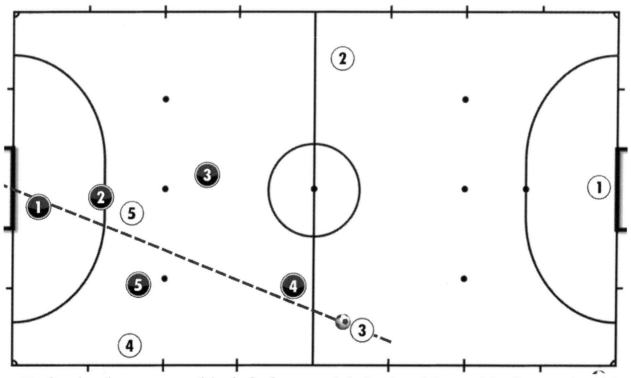

Defender has to put his left foot and left shoulder a bit forward. This

futsalicodvd.com | Youtube.com/futsalico_ENG | instagram@futsalico_ENG

help us to avoid the situation, where white nr.3 moves into the middle (to his strongest side and potentially dangerous shooting position). In case, in white nr.3 still decides to go towards the middle, black nr.4 (defender) will have much better chance to take the ball away from opponent anyway.

TACTICAL TRAP NR.3

Turning opponent's attack towards the flank

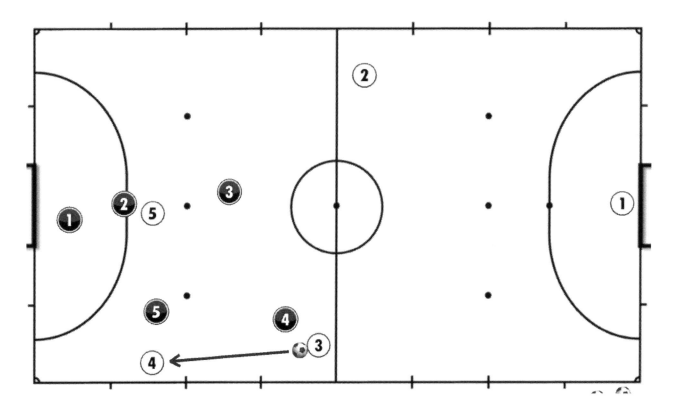

How and why you should turn your opponent towards the flank? Take a look at the scheme above. Such a position of black nr.4 motivates white nr.3 to move to the left - to his (or her) weakest side. This position also move our opponent towards the flank and it can be useful for defense regardless of which foot of opponent is the strongest.

The main objective of a defender in this case is to move an opponent to a certain zone. Why may this tactic be useful for a defending side? Main risk here is the fact, that from the center our opponent might have way more potential directions of attack. Let us take a look at the next scheme. It will allow us to see possible direction, attack might take.

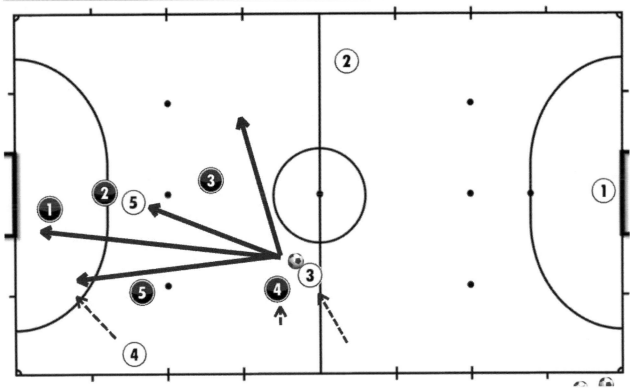

You can see, that white nr.3 has **four possible directions** of play from this position: he can pass the ball to the right flank, connect with the pivot in the middle, shoot at goal or play to the nearest post. Each of these options is very dangerous.

Position in the middle of the pitch usually gives an attacking player many different options and a corridor for a shot. You also have to remember, that every decent futsaler can take an accurate shot from any position, which is closer to the goal, than 12 meters.

For those players, who have a very good shooting skill, 12 meters is not a distance at all. They are capable of scoring from such distance under almost every angle. Now imagine, you have an opponent with a very good shooting skill inside 12 meters to the goal and in the middle zone - just in front of the goal (with almost zero angle). Every defense must try to avoid that.

This is the main reason, why most teams prefer not to allow an attacking opponent into the middle section of the pitch.

TACTICAL TRAP NR.4

Turning opponent's attack towards the center

We already understood, that "moving" an opponent away from the center might be very useful. Although, there is a tactical strategy, which is based on moving opponent's away from the flanks and into the middle. Why would that be useful?

First of all, if futsal was so simple, it wouldn't be so exciting. The thing is, that there is no strict system, where it could be said: "do that" and "don't do that" and you win the match. At the beginning of any futsal game you can never tell for 100%, who would win the match, just based on what tactics teams apply and what players they have in their disposal.

Each and every tactic has it's pros and cons, it's benefits and it's flaws. Each idea might work, each strategy might get you to a victory. That is why I always encourage every coach to try their ideas. Some of them might work, some of them might not work, but each coach has a right to choose his own strategy. Remember: coach is only judged by the result!

My job as an author of this book is to give you as much information as I can about pros and cons of different tactics, show you the nature of futsal and this way - to get you as ready and as knowledgeable as possible. Everything else is up to you. You know your team better than anyone else.

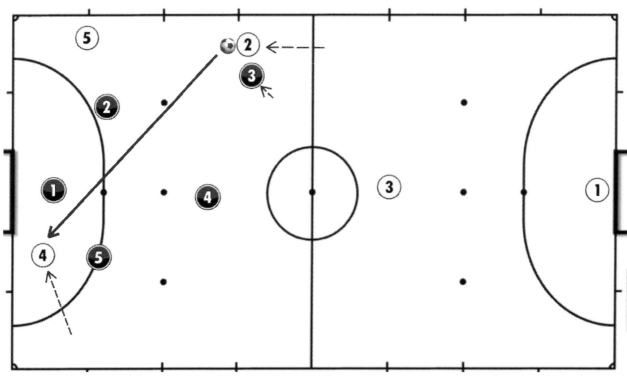

So why would a defensive team might need a strategy, the main idea of which is turning opponent to the center? This kind of strategy is useful in those cases, when, for example, opponents tend to shoot from the flanks.

There are players, who like to push the ball down the flank (right-footed players on right flanks and left-footed players on left flanks) and shoot. There are teams, which are using flanks, to pass the ball from there towards the far post, where another opponent's player arrives to finish (like it's shown on the previous scheme).

These kind is players are better to deal with in the center. These kind of teams are also better to move to the center and with after creating a compact defensive block and deal with them there. Players, which tend to shoot from flanks, when moved to the center, would have to put the ball on their weakest foot. This way you can stop them from making dangerous shots form flanks and make them play on their weakest sides.

Now comes the "**how**" part. Let's take an example:

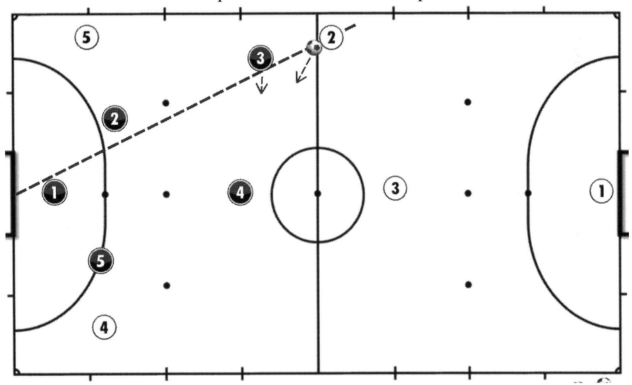

This is a typical case of a right-footed player with a good shooting skill and on the right flank. Ideal position for him. So let's say, defender's decided to move this opponent towards the center to get him away from the right flank and possible dangerous shot with his right (strongest) foot.

To make an opponent with the ball to move to the center, defender has to put his left foot and left shoulder a bit forward and approach his opponent from the flank.

Black nr.4 must be very focused too. If his (or her) partner (black nr.3) makes the opponent with the ball move towards the middle, black nr.4

must take couple of steps to his left, towards the middle. This would protect the middle section, making defensive system much more compact. It will also allow to "meet" opponent with the ball in case, if black nr.3 gets outplayed. The most important though is that this kind of adjustment of positioning by black nr.4 would allow him (or her) to block the passing line from white nr.2 to white nr.4 (next scheme):

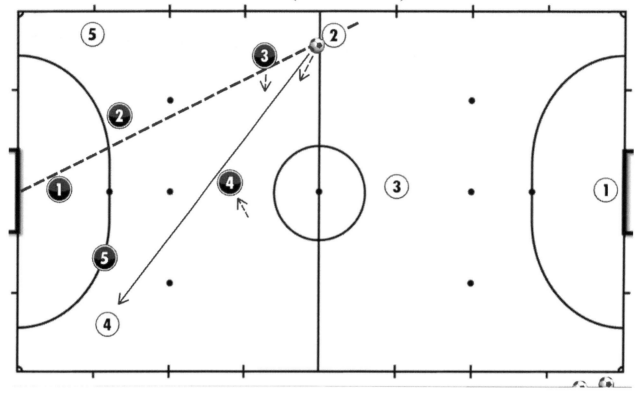

Do not forget also, that if white nr.2 moves to the middle, he can play the pass to the center (pivot position), like it's shown in the next scheme:

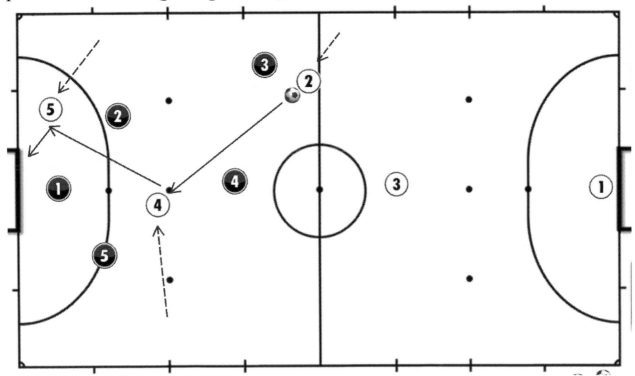

This is why black nr.4 should move in the middle and be aware of these scenarios. He will be the one responsible for any pass, which goes through the middle (not black nr.3).

So now you know, different tactical strategies, different traps, which can be set by defense in order to achieve certain goals. Next thing to do is decide, **which tactic is the most suitable for which situation.** Remember, that opponents are different, so tactics might be changing from match to match.

I would like to give you some tips, which would help you understand, which strategy to use and when.

Analysis of your opponent

Before facing any opponent, at least, you have to understand, what is their style of play. Do they like to use flanks? Do they prefer to attack through the middle? Are they using a counter-attacking style or maybe they prefer combinational, well-prepared attackers and take they time.

What are their players like? Are there any good shooters? What foot is their strongest? In which positions they lose the ball more often and what are positions, they pose their biggest threat etc. This information will give you a perspective and a clearer look at, what is going on.

Analyze you own team

At first you must understand, are you players even good enough to be applying your (coach's) idea on the pitch. For example, if their fitness levels are very low, then in 2-3 minutes on the pitch, they will be so tired, that they will forget any tactic and any strategy. Even if they would still remember it, they won't have any strength to apply it.

You also have to analyze, how good of a keeper you have. Is he capable of dealing with long shots, for example? If he is a very good shot stopper, then your team may not be afraid of shots from flanks, we talked about previously. All you have to do in this case is make sure, that you covered the far post (in case, if there is another opponent, trying to tap it in). The fact, the your keeper is dealing with long shots with ease, can allow you not to be turning your opponents towards the middle, for example. This fact will give you more tactical options.

On the contrary, if your keeper is a very poor shot-stopper (and there is no way, you can exchange him with another), then the main focus of your defensive strategy should be on not allowing any dangerous shots. This way you might have to turn your opponent's with the ball towards they weakest foot, regardless, of where they might end-up (in the middle or on the flank). The most important in this case would be stopping them from shooting from their strongest foot.

Let's say, you have very fit players at your disposal, very experienced and skillful. This can give you tactical flexibility. Now you can instruct your players to adapt tactical approaches during the game to a certain situation. For example, they can be playing against one opponent in one way and with another opponent - in another way. The best thing about skillful, experienced and tactically well equipped player is that they can adapt to a game situation and change strategy on the go - according to, what is happening at this very moment.

Use drills to help players learn each strategy

This is what many coaches (captains, managers or playing-coaches) tend to forget about. It's not enough to explain your players, who to play and when. They have to develop game habits (muscle memory), which will allow to keep playing correctly even, when a player is tired, under stress or in a hurry.

futsalicodvd.com | Youtube.com/futsalico_ENG | instagram@futsalico_ENG

BIGGEST DEFENSIVE CHALLENGES

HOW TO PLAY AGAINST A PIVOT

In this section of the book we are going to learn, how to play against pivots and also take a look at specific futsal scenarios. Playing against a pivot is one of the hardest challenges for any defender. If an opponent has a good pivot, it's always difficult to keep him from scoring. This is why I decided to include this chapter in my book. We will take different situations and divide them into 4 topics (4 biggest challenges):

1. **Playing against a central pivot**
2. **Playing against a flank pivot**
3. **Exchanging opponent's players**
4. **Playing against a quick and skillful opponent**

First of all, let's start with the main concepts regarding the defense against a pivot. Pivot is a lone attacking player, who plays most of his time on the opponent's half of the pitch. When his team attacks, he prefers to go far on the opponent's half and wait for a pass there.

One of the main skills of the pivot is first touch. He should be able to open-up for the pass and makes sure, he gets the ball under control with the first touch. Some might think, that the main skill of the pivot is dribbling and shooting. I assure you, it's not. He should be able to shield the ball from opponents with his body and find his teammate with a good pass. There for most important skills of the pivot are first touch, shielding and passing.

So if you have a player in your team, who has such skills on a good level, you might consider making him your pivot. Pivot is usually used in formations **1-3-1** and **1-1-2-1**. Therefore, if you are using a pivot, you should be ready and have knowledge to play these formations. I have a video course on futsalicodvd.com, which focuses of explaining all futsal formations. Check it out.

Here is **formation 1-3-1**, where player nr.2 is a pivot:

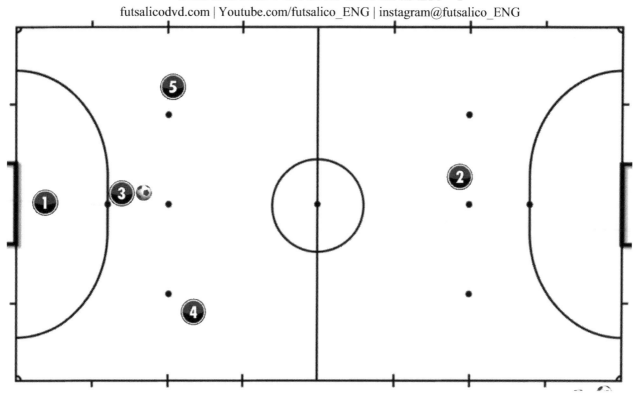

Here is a **formation 1-1-2-1**, where player nr.2 is a pivot:

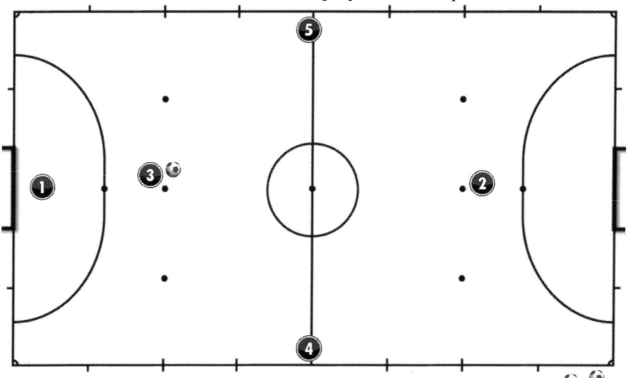

There are some tactics, which include two pivots. Although we won't be wasting our time and focus for them in this book. Spanish futsal club Barcelona, for example, has Brazilian Ferrao and Spanish national team player - Lozano. Both players are pivots. Sometimes they are on the pitch together. It doesn't mean, though, that both of them are simultaneously playing on opponent's half, but still attacking tactical approach changes very much. If you want to dig deep in the topic of a futsal pivot, there is a

futsalicodvd.com | Youtube.com/futsalico_ENG | instagram@futsalico_ENG

video course on futsalicodvd.com, which tells you all you need to know about futsal pivots.

HOW TO PLAY AGAINST A CENTRAL PIVOT

Here is an example of a situation, when an opponent uses central pivot (white nr.5):

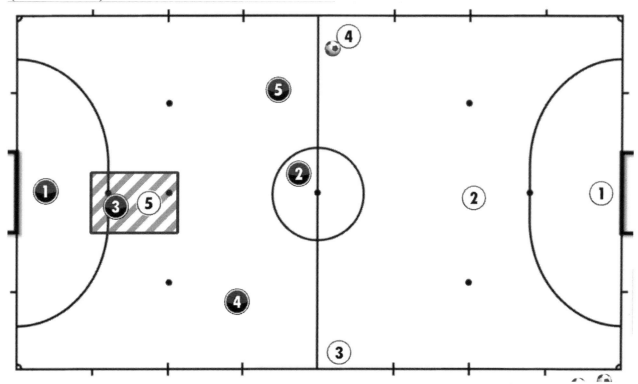

Main job of the black nr.3, who has to play against the pivot - prevent him from facing our goal. The thing is, that a pivot is closer than 12 meters to the goals. Everything, which is lower than 12 meters, is a distance, from which a player with a decent shot can score. If an attacking player has a good shooting skill, it won't be a big problem for him to hit the target from there.

Central pivot is also dangerous, because he is receiving balls right in front of our goal (in the center). Therefore, if he turns, he is immediately in a perfect position for a shot. All he needs to do now is take a shot.

Considering all mentioned above, defender (black nr.3), has to:

- **Keep safe distance** (1.5-2m) to the Pivot
- **Spread his feet** a bit, bent them in knees and find a good balance. This will allow a defender to react to whatever a pivot is up to. This body position will allow a defender to block the shot in case if the pivot turns.
- **Put one hand in front of himself** and touch a pivot's back (or hip). In order for this touch to be according to the laws of the game, a defender has to touch, but not push or grab. Position himself at certain

angle (putting one foot a and shoulder a bit forward). Ideally defender's feet should repeat the position of pivot's feet.

Should a defender try and take the ball away from a pivot? I would put it this way: taking the ball away from a pivot is not the most important job of a defender, who plays against this pivot. Of course, if you are up against a pivot and you are given an opportunity to tackle and win the ball, you should use it.

This might happen if a pivot makes a bad turn, let's the ball go too far away from him, makes a bad first touch etc. Although, any defender, who plays against a pivot, should know, that his **main job is not to let a pivot to face the goal with the ball at his feet.** Because, as I said earlier, from this position any shot is a potential goal.

Picture above shows you the outcome of the situation, when a defender let's a pivot turn and face the goal.

While one defender doesn't allow opponent's pivot to turn, other defenders should be watching the opponent's players and make sure, that they do not receive a pass from a pivot! If a pivot manages to make a pass to his teammate, then the one, who is responsible for the receiver, should position himself between the ball and the goal. I illustrated this situation in the next scheme:

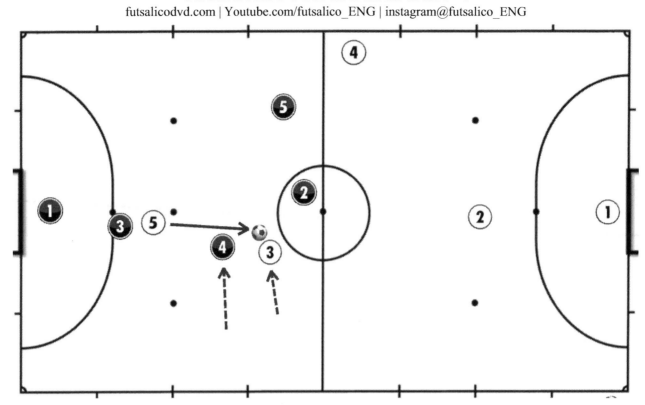

After white nr.5 (pivot) plays the ball to his teammate (white nr.3), a defender, who is responsible for white nr.3, immediately positions himself between the player with the ball and the goal. This way black nr.4 is able to block a potential shot.

futsalicodvd.com | Youtube.com/futsalico_ENG | instagram@futsalico_ENG

HOW TO PLAY AGAINST A FLANK PIVOT

What you do defensively against a central pivot and against a flank pivot is usually almost the same. There are couple of nuances, though, a defender has to understand.

The main job a defender, who plays against a flank pivot, is (just as against a central pivot) - prevent a pivot from facing our goal with the ball at his feet.

The only exception is, that, when working against flank pivot, defender has some space to retreat.

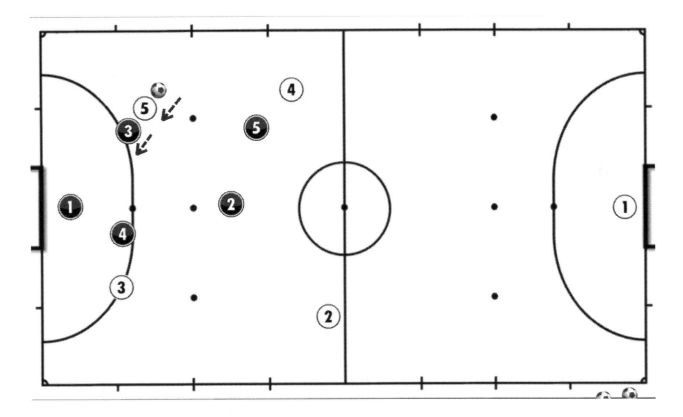

Usually good pivots are able to hit the ball well with both of their feet. Although, there are pivots (and especially it's relevant to amateur or youth futsal), who can only hit the ball well with one of their feet.

A pivot, who prefers to play with only his strongest foot, such a player would still be very dangerous on a central pivot's position. Because, wherever he turns (even if he turns to his weakest foot), he is still dangerous. The reason for this is the fact, that he is just in front of the goal.

Now, regarding the flank pivot, the main danger for a defender is, if a pivot turns to his strongest foot. The situation, when a pivot turns to his weakest foot is less dangerous, because there will still be a good distance to a goal.

As a coach (captain, manager etc.) you should consider these factors and choose according tactics for the game. As a defender, you should also remember about these nuances, when you are up against a pivot on the flank. Some defenders try to provoke a pivot to go to the side of his weakest foot. This gives a defender an opportunity to engage in a tackle, when pivot turns like that. This might be a good moment for a defender to take the ball away from the pivot. All a defender needs after he turned a pivot to his weakest side is to time his tackle well.

As I said previously, the ability of a pivot to turn is not the main problem. It's way worse for a defender, if a pivot knows, how to find his partners with a good pass. If such a pass is timed and implemented well, then it's not going to be the pivot, who a defending team should be afraid of. It's his partner, who opens up for a shot. The next scheme illustrate such a situation:

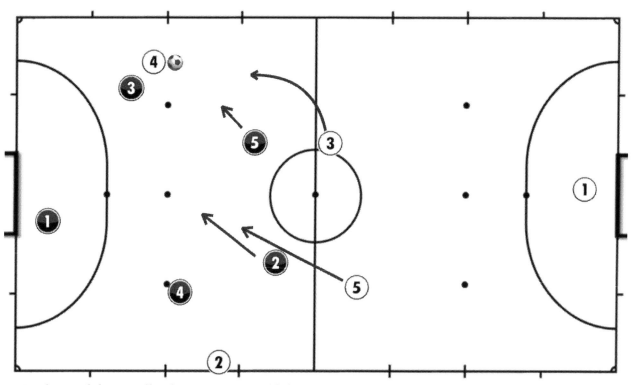

Being able to find a partner with an accurate and well-timed pass is the main weapon of a pivot. Smart and skillful futsal pivot knows, how to gather opponent's players around him and create spaces for other partners.

HOW TO SWITCH COVER

This question is very popular amongst the subscribers of my Youtube channel (youtube.com/futsalico_eng). "In personal cover tactic, can I give the opponent, which I am covering, to another teammate at some point or should I follow him all over the pitch no matter what?" When I was planning topics of this book, I made a decision, that the answer to this question should be included in here. This is a question, which is asked by many amateur futsal players and they have the right to know the answer to it.

First thing's first: you can not "give" an opponent to your teammate! If you are using a personal cover tactics, then as a defender you can only "take" an opponent. That means, that if there is no signal from your teammate, that he wants to "take" your player, then you should continue following your opponent everywhere he goes.

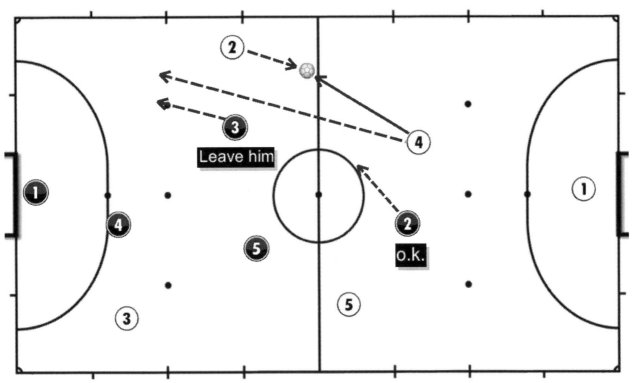

Take a look at the scheme above. Attacking team's players are making a rotation. White nr.4 is the last player (closest to his goal) and white nr.5 is on the right flank. White nr.4 passes the ball to white nr.5 and they exchange their positioning. White nr.4 moves to the right flank into a position of white nr.5. White nr.5, on the other hand, receives the ball and instead of teammate (white nr.4) becomes the last player (closest to his goal).

This exchange of positions is very popular if futsal. Therefore, professional players, who are defending such a situation, oftentimes are not following their respective players all they way, but instead - they exchange them. So if we imagine, that in the illustrated situation we have a professional team in defense, then black nr.2 and black nr.3 would just remain on their positions. Without saying a word.

That is possible only, when both players are experienced, tactically equipped and can read the game well. For black nr.2, for example, it would be enough just to take a look at black nr.5 to see, that he is getting back into a position of a last player. Therefore black nr.2 can just switch from white nr.4 to white nr.5. Professional player would also be sure, that his teammate (also a pro) also understands this and therefore would just switch from white nr.5 to white nr.4.

For amateur players it's not the case, though. They don't often see, how the play goes. More often, then not, amateurs cannot read the game well. Therefore, amateurs should be always talking to each other on the pitch. Always signaling.

When I work with teams, which are beginners and amateurs, who never trained in futsal and do not have much tactical knowledge, I always tell my players, that, when you play a personal cover, your respective opponent is your responsibility. That is always, that is all the time. You have to follow him wherever he goes. The only situation, where you can leave him is when you are leaving him to your teammate, who just gave you a **signal** to do it. Without a signal, continue to follow your respective opponent.

Take a look at the previous picture again, please. You can see, that black nr.3 is giving a signal to the teammate in front of him. This signal tells black nr.2, that he may leave his player now, everything is under control. That signal also means, that black nr.3 is switching his attention to another opponent and that means - black nr.2 has to do the same (now his responsibility is to cover white nr.5).

The kind of defensive tactic, which allows frequent switching of responsibilities, is called switching system. Although some switching can be also used is personal cover and some times even in zonal system.

For example, if defending team is using personal cover and there is a situation, when opponents are switching positions too obviously, defenders may easily switch responsibilities. It's just rational. Although switching always should be done with a signal. Want to learn to do the switching without signaling, wait for 20 or 30 games and it will happen eventually. But start with developing a habit to communicate in such situations.

HOW TO PLAY AGAINST QUICK AND SKILLFUL OPPONENT

This topic is also very important to discuss, because it's about defending one on one against your respective opponent. It should be said, that the way of playing against quick and skillful opponent will differ, depending on what defensive tactic (zonal, personal cover, mixed or switching) is used. The book, you are reading now, is about individual (one on one) defense. Therefore the best defensive system to illustrate my point is personal cover.

In the first part of this book we already discussed, how and when you should be tackling a player or intercepting a pass. We talked about the necessary conditions for a tackle or interception and how you can read (see) them.

In this section, though, we are concentrating on defending against skillful and quick players. Therefore we may have to adjust (or bend) some of the methods of defense, which we already know.

The main advantage of a skilled and fast futsaler is his ability to make quick and unpredicted decisions. This kind of players love and can use a free space and their time on the ball effectively. Therefore, main job of a defender is to, first of all - give such players as little time and space, as possible. Second - get into positions, which will allow you to react the best way possible to whatever your opponent does.

Therefore, when playing against skillful opponent, it is important for a defender to be able to take a correct position on the pitch, when opponent doesn't have the ball yet, when he is about to receive the ball and when he is already with the ball. These are things, we discussed already, although in this chapter I will try to give you a fresher look to these situations and explain to you, how you can apply your knowledge the best way possible. You will need to be at your very best in defense, because you are facing ultimate attacker.

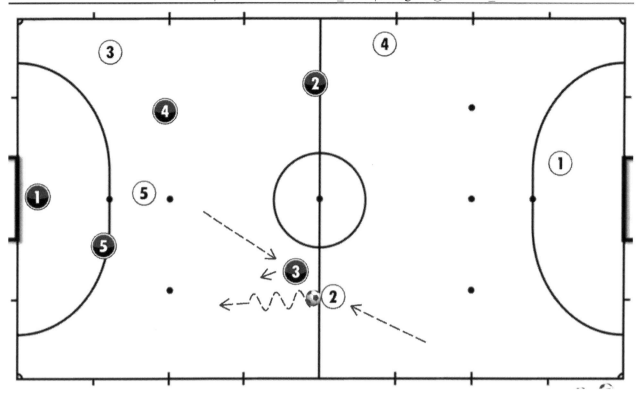

If it comes to dealing with a quick and skillful player, a defender must get closer to such and opponent only, when all necessary conditions are met. Scheme above shows you an incorrect positioning by the defender. Black nr.3 made a bad decision and got too close to a player with the ball. As a result, attacking player easily got by a defender.

Let's start with the list of necessary conditions to tackle a quick and skillful opponent. At least one of the following conditions should be met before engaging in a fight for the ball. First condition - bad first touch by an attacking player. Giving the fact, that we are talking about a skillful player, bad first touch won't happen a lot. Most of the time, the receiver will get the ball under control inside two first touches. Although, these players also make mistakes. The job of the defender is to be able to read it and act accordingly and in time.

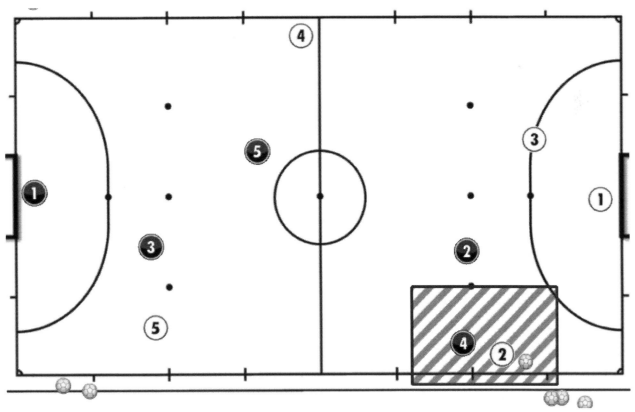

Second condition - lack of space (scheme above). Attacking player (with the ball) has to operate within a strictly limited space and time. It's better fo a defender, if everything is happening near the side line.

Third condition - player with the ball is turned with his back towards a defender and there is no one to pass the ball to (scheme above). This happens regularly in an amateur futsal. Usually the reason for this is, that teammates are not creating passing lines for a player with the ball. It may even be, that teammates do not know, how to create passing lines correctly. The job of a defender is to be able to see it in time and put pressure on a player with the ball.

If you are a coach, I suggest, you teach your players to be able to see this kind of situations (when a player with the ball is turned with his back and there is no one to pass the ball to). In amateur and youth league this ability might let you win load of balls, which could give you loads of opportunities to score. This ability alone can mean, that you are going to have a lot of points won.

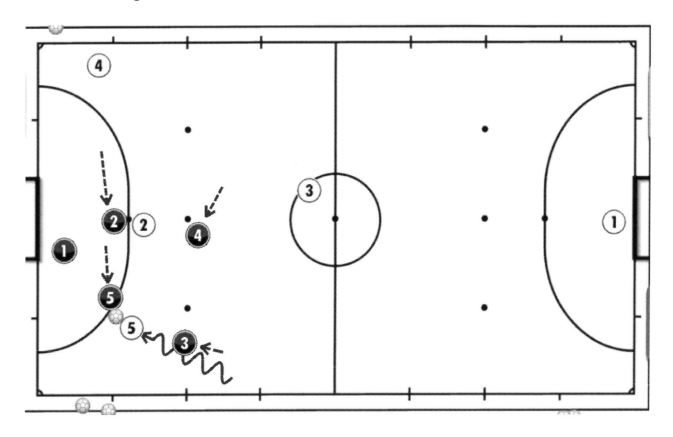

Condition nr.4 is having a **support** by your teammates (scheme above). The main idea is that, before attacking a skillful opponent with the ball, defensive system must allow some kind of a plan B. In case, if a defender, who is up against a player with the ball, does not succeed.

Scheme above shows us a situation, where a high level of skill allowed white nr.5 to outplay black nr.3. Defensive system (positioning of all four defenders) in this case allowed black nr.5 to be able to provide support in time. As a result, black nr.5 hits the ball out of play, preventing a dangerous situation and letting his team to reconstruct the defense. This was possible only because defensive team had a plan B: every defender was in a position, which allowed him to support his teammate.

Note, that the **biggest danger** for a defender, who is up against a skillful and quick opponent is getting in a situation, where:

- **Opponent makes a perfect first touch**, gets the ball under full control and quickly gets in an active attacking position (with attacking intent). Active attacking position means, that player with has the ball under control, in front of him, faces opponent's goals and already started moving towards it (next scheme).

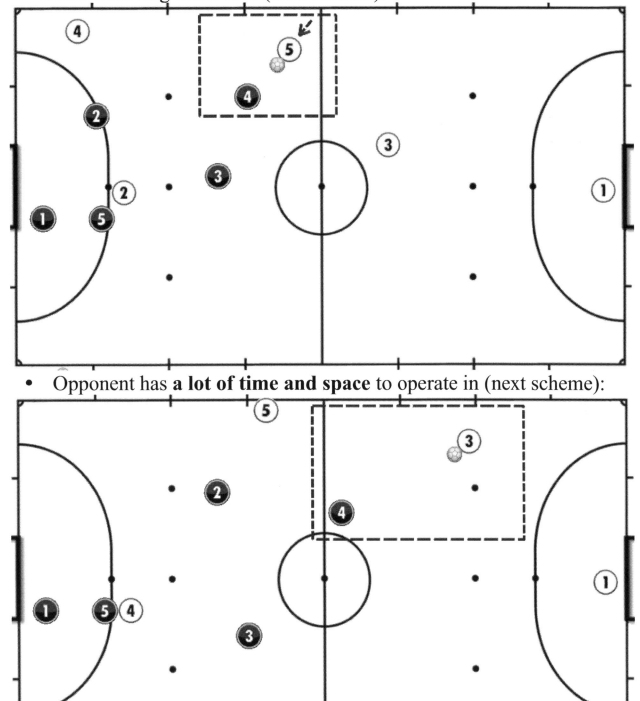

- Opponent has **a lot of time and space** to operate in (next scheme):

- opponent **has several options** for a pass (more than one passing lines are provided by his teammates) - next scheme:

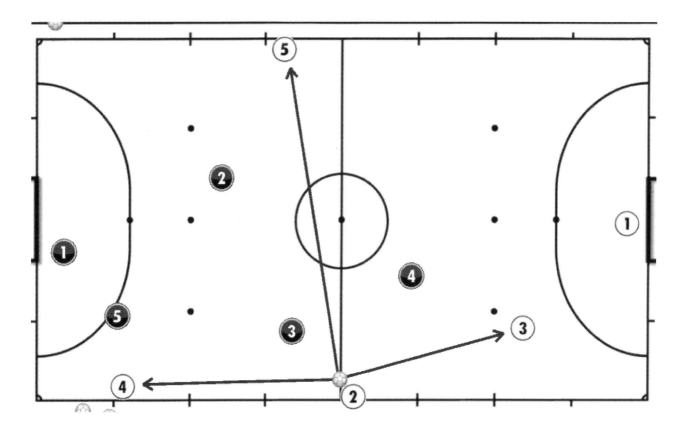

If a skillful player in such position (previous scheme) has multiple options for a pass, he immediately becomes much more dangerous just because of that. To tackle him at this point would not be a very wise decision. The only fact, that an opponent has three options for a pass, already means that the defensive system is very poorly constructed.

This also means, that collective defensive attention is spread and has no focus. There are too many potential dangers for a defense at this point. To many potential direction of attack and options for attacking players. That automatically means, that black nr.3 should not be expecting any support by his teammates if case, if he loses his respective player (white nr.2).

Too many passing lines are a good indicator for a black nr.3 not to throw himself into a reckless tackle. Instead he should take a defensive position (1.5-2m away from a player with the ball) and wait. If white nr.2 pushes it towards black team's goal, then black nr.2 has to get back too, while keeping the distance and staying on the line between the ball and the center of his goal.

The situation, illustrated on a previous picture, actually shows a good a example of how the existence of many passing lines not just makes a skillful player with the ball dangerous. It also means, that all his teammates become as dangerous too.

The same thing happens, when your opponent has a skillful pivot. When such a player receive the ball in your half, it's not just the pivot himself, who becomes dangerous. All his teammates becomes as much dangerous as he is or maybe - even more dangerous.

In previous chapters we already talked about a pivot and how to deal with him. I would like to demonstrate another example, though, so you could understand, how dangerous it can be, when a skillful player with the ball at his feet has multiple options for a pass.

Here is a situation, when **a pivot receives the ball in the heart of our defense:**

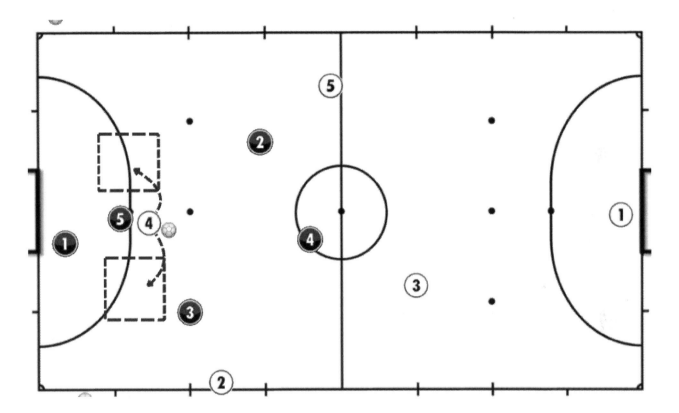

This is a case, when a pivot doesn't really have any options for a pass. Therefore the biggest danger for a defense is a pivot's turn to one of the sides. This turn would give him a necessary corridor for a shot. In this case all pivot's partners are covered by defenders.

Knowing, that white nr.4 only has and option to turn (and doesn't have an option for a pass), for a black defender nr.5 it would be much easier to control the pivot.

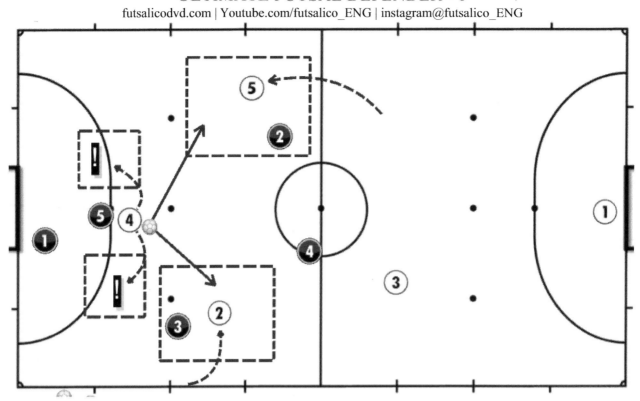

Scheme above shows us, how incorrect positioning of black nr.3 and black nr.2 allowed two of white team's players to create passing lines for a pivot. Now pivot has four possible options for a pass. This means, that black nr.5 (who is up against a pivot) now has to deal with four possible scenarios. This spreads his attention and make it more difficult for him to defend.

In case, if a pass goes to white nr.5, black nr.5 will have to go out to provide support. Black nr.3 or a keeper would have to switch to covering a pivot now. So the fact, that pivot had so many options to make a pass, now created additional problems for black nr.5 and for the whole defensive team. That's, what can happen, it a skillful player has a ball at his feet and his partners are open for a pass.

- **Defender doesn't have a support** (and defensive system is poorly constructed too) - next scheme:

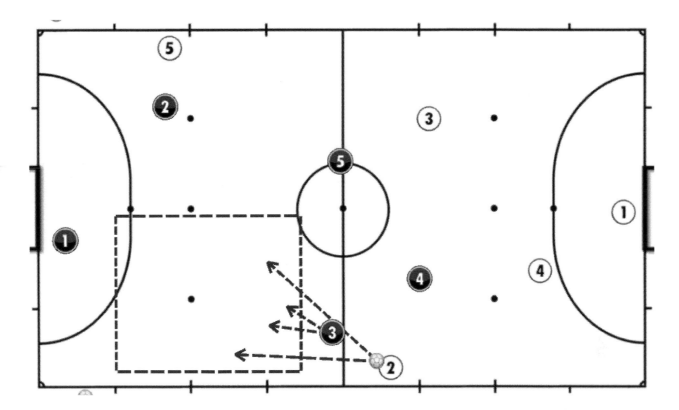

Picture above shows you a situation, when black team is so spread out (black nr.2 should have been closer to the middle, black nr.4 - lower etc.), that black nr.3 is left with no support. There is a big space behind him, which can easily be used by an attacking team.

At the end of this chapter I will provide you an example from futsal team Russia and the tactic, they are using very often. Robinho being a very quick and skillful player, loves to use his skill to the maximum and was able to help his team many times during trouble.

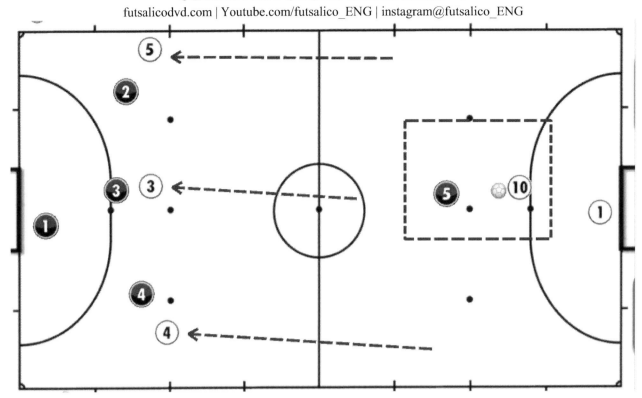

On the scheme above Robinho is white nr.10. He is **intentionally** left "at home" (as the last player), when his teammates are going far forward (on the opponent's half). His opponents are not creating for Robinho no passing lines. The main idea of such strategy is relying on Robinho's ability to outplay a defender. Therefore creating a 4v3 situation and capitalizing on it.

There is a certain risk in this strategy. Although in many cases it can be justified. Robinho's skill gives a coaching stuff big flexibility. I will definitely talk about attacking side of such a tactic in one of my ebooks on attack. In here, though, we are focusing on a defensive side.

So how should a defender be playing against such a master with the ball? There are two options. Decision to prefer one or another should be based on such factors as the score, level skill of an opponent's player, overall level of an attacking team and on the philosophy of a coach, his idea and intuition.

One option would be pressuring Robinho very high up the pitch (as far away from our goal as possible). The main risk in this case would be, that Robinho outplays a defender and opponent gets numerical advantage in attack (next scheme):

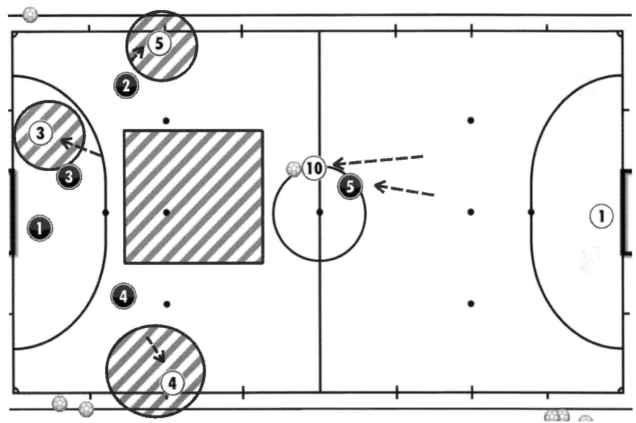

The benefit of such defensive tactic (high pressure) is a chance for a defending team to get the ball away from Robinho very close to his goal. If a defending team is winning at this point, then any additional goal against Robinho's team might just mean the guaranteed victory.

This is the main reason, why high pressure at this point might be a good idea. Therefore, if, for example, a defender, who is up against Robinho is very experienced and quick too. That would give him a bigger chance to take the ball away from Robinho. This kind of defender would also be able (in case, if Robinho outplays him) to catch up with Robinho and regain his positioning quickly before an attacking team is able to use a situation in their favor.

If your team does not possess such a skillful and experienced defender, may be you should not pressure a player like Robinho too high up the pitch. May be in this case you would have to start defending from the middle line of the pitch (on your half). Construct a compact defense and wait for it. In this case, if Robinho outplays one player, another would be able to come to the rescue.

If a defender up front is outplayed, then defending team should adapt to it. According to what tactic is prepared for this case, a defensive team can, for example, apply switching (next scheme):

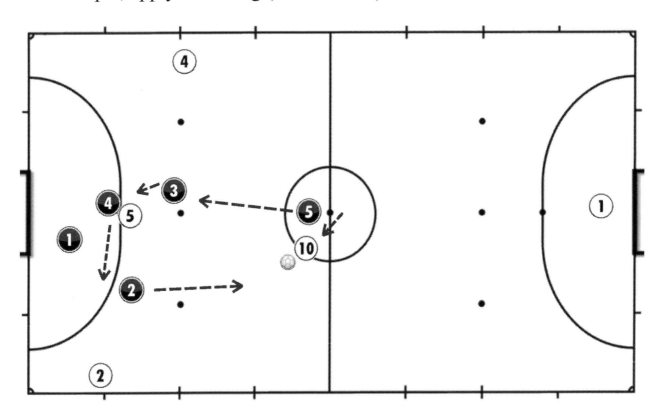

Supporting player (black nr.2) comes out to meet Robinho. Other players are moving in a counterclockwise movement. Black nr.4 moves to the right, black nr.3 gets a bit closer to his goal and takes white nr.5. Black nr.5 (the one, who was outplayed in the first place) doesn't lose his time and follow Robinho. He just get's back, covers the middle zone and watches white nr.4.

There is another strategy too. Outplayed black nr.5 has to follow Robinho anyway. All other defensive players keep watching their respective opponents (next scheme):

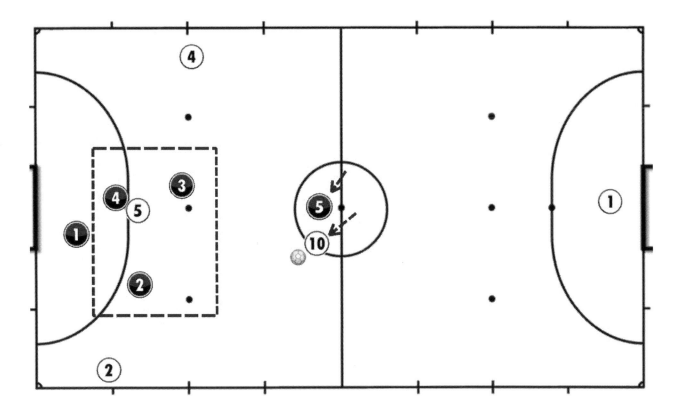

For me this tactic would be an option too in case if I had to play against a player like Robinho. The thing is, that such attacking strategy, which is used by an opponent, focuses on creating a numeric advantage and then capitalizing on it. The idea is to outplay one defender and make other defenders change their positions and lose their respective players for a bit. When defenders change positions, opponent's players for some moment of time are left without a cover. This is a moment, when the player with the ball makes a pass to one of them.

This is why, if you are switching, you have to do it very quickly and correctly. Therefore, if defenders are not switching, but instead - stay with their players (and defender, who got outplayed, tries to get back to the play with the ball), they does not allow any passing line. The only thing, Robinho can do now is shoot.

What is more dangerous: to let a player like Robinho shoot or to let him pass? This is a question, you are going to have to answer on your our. You are the one, who knows your team better than anyone else. I am just giving you different options and show you pros and cons.

Here's something to analyze. For example, you have a very good keeper, who deals with shots with ease. At the same time my players are very good defensively. This gives me assurance, that in case if some of them gets outplayed, he will be able to regain his positioning very fast. That kind of skill set of my team, would make me instruct them not to switch, but instead - remain on their positions if the front player is outplayed.

If my keeper is not that good with stopping shots and my players are not that good defensively in one on one situations, I would prefer to use a zonal defense and make them cover each other (leave their players and provide support for a teammate) in case, if one of them is outplayed.

The last thing you have to remember about, when you are up against a quick and skillful player, is that usually **such players feel uncomfortable against an aggressive defender.** Aggressive means - very **focused, coolheaded and skillful in tackling.** The one, who likes to put pressure and knows, how to do it. The one, who does not allow an opponent much space and time on a ball.

Aggressive doesn't mean, he fouls a lot. On the contrary - he knows, how to time his tackles and what is the difference between a constant, controlled pressure and throwing himself on an opponent recklessly.

CONCLUSION

In this book we talked about individual defensive actions in different situations. Information was divided into three blocks: opponent without the ball, opponent, who is about to receive a ball, opponent with the ball. We also discussed some tactical defensive traps and learned to face biggest defensive challenges.

You have to remember the most important thing - success always hides in small detail. Therefore you should works on improving each and every small thing: positioning on the pitch, body position, vision, defensive intent, psychological approach to a game, focusing on most important objectives, improving your drills and overall training process. Professional and successful players are the ones, who improved every tactical and technical nuance and managed to turn the result into a habit.

Get back to this book, when there is a need. Each chapter is designed in a way, that it let's you address a certain issue, you might deal with. Take your time in futsal and do not try to learn everything in the first year. Take it step by step.

I thank you for purchasing this book. Hope, it was useful for you. This is the first book of the series called **"Ultimate Futsal Defender"** and will include 3 or four books. Next book will focus on individual skills of defenders, way to improve them (with the help of drills) and more specific situations.

Please, subscribe to my Youtube channel on **youtube.com/futsalico_eng** and follow me on Instagram: **Instagram.com/futsalico_eng**. This is not only the place to get a lot of free futsal content, but also - to stay informed on new releases of my books and video courses and discounts.

Keep it safe. Stay healthy. See you soon!

LINKS

Let's stay in touch!

Instagram.com/**futsalico_eng**
Twitter.com/**futsalico_com**
Youtube.com/**futsalico_eng**
Facebook.com/**futsalico**

My books and video courses - futsalicodvd.com

Printed in Great Britain
by Amazon